Police Governance
in
England and Wales

Cavendish
Publishing
Limited

London • Sydney

Police Governance in England and Wales

Arthur Brown, BSc (Econ),
Former Police Inspector, Cheshire Constabulary
Lecturer in Law and Public Administration,
West Cheshire College

Cavendish
Publishing
Limited

London • Sydney

First published in Great Britain 1998 by Cavendish Publishing Limited,
The Glass House, Wharton Street, London, WC1X 9PX.
Telephone: 0171-278 8000 Facsimile: 0171-278 8080
e-mail: info@cavendishpublishing.com
Visit our Home Page on http://www.cavendishpublishing.com

Brown, Arthur
Police Governance in England and Wales
1. Police – England 2. Police – Wales
I. Title
345.4'2'052

ISBN 1-85941-395-1

Printed and bound in Great Britain

Foreword

I am very pleased to have been asked to write a foreword for this handbook.

Great changes have been introduced into the police service in recent years, resulting in much greater centralised control and a consequential reduction in Local Authority involvement in police matters.

This handbook deals with the organisation, financing and control of the police service as contained in the Police Act 1996. It sets out the constitutional position of a constable, details the limits on his powers and the actions that can be taken against him, within the service and by private persons, if he exceeds his powers.

Being completely up to date, it gives details, not only of the police service but of those organisations with close affinity to the police, such as the Security Service and the newly created national services – the National Criminal Intelligence Service, the National Crime Squad and the Police Information Technology Organisation.

Topics not covered in other police books are dealt with. For example, the financing of the police service under the provisions in the Police Act 1996 is covered, supplemented by an account of the functions of the Audit Commission in this regard.

Similarly, the procedure for dealing with complaints against the actions of individual police officers are covered, but supplemented by a chapter on civil remedies under the law of tort.

Explanation of relevant cases is given in appropriate places throughout the text. A full reference list of statutes and a table of cases is provided.

Anyone wishing to know anything about the police organisation and how the service and its members are controlled and financed need go no further than this book, which is written clearly and simply so that it will be readily understood by the layperson with no knowledge of the subject. Equally, it will be of great value to any police officer wanting to know 'where he stands'.

GE Fenn, CBE, QPM, LLB, DL
former Chief Constable, Cheshire Constabulary
October 1997

Preface

Since 1994 several new statutory provisions concerning the governance of provincial police forces have come into effect. A series of judicial decisions have also affected this area.

The handbook is politically neutral, as it is confined to matters of the law, including descriptions of how the law has been interpreted in some particular situations.

The text outlines the legal authorities that govern the provincial police forces of England and Wales. The references to statutes and judicial decisions are necessarily brief in a document of this size and readers needing more detailed information will have to consult the original authorities. I have included appropriate references to facilitate further research by readers.

The most recent statutes concerned with policing activities are included, with the legal provisions being described in straight forward language. However, references are provided throughout the text in the following format:

- section 2 (with no further amplification) – Police Act 1996
- section 2 PA 1997 – Police Act 1997
- section 2 SS Act – Security Service Act 1989 as extended by the Security Service Act 1996

Other references to statutes are given in full.

Cases are referred to by name and date with detailed references being included in the table of cases.

The handbook is designed to be understandable to the non-lawyer and at the same time providing a handy reference source for those more learned in the subject matter. It should be of use to members of police forces, police authorities and others having a professional concern with the governance of the police. Additionally, it would be a valuable tool for students studying such subjects as constitutional and administrative law, public administration, criminology, politics and other allied subjects.

I would like to pay thanks to Mr GE Fenn who took the trouble to read the text and then drew my attention to additional items of information, all of which enhanced the quality of the handbook. I have valued his encouragement and example over many years.

Arthur Brown
October 1997

Contents

Part IV   93

10 Her Majesty's Inspectors of Constabulary 95

11 The Audit Commission 99

12 Control by the Judiciary 103

Table of Cases

Table of Statutes

Major statutes concerning police forces are shown in bold type.

Part I

The powers, responsibilities and functions
of members of police forces and
others associated with the policing role

1   Prerogative Power, the Queen's Peace and Individual Rights

The beginnings

The Crown enjoys the authority of the royal prerogative which consists of special dignities, powers and privileges under the authority of the common law. This power places the Crown above all other citizens and it includes the authority to enforce the Queen's peace throughout her realm.

The most basic definition of the Queen's peace is that any person who breaks the laws of the land can be taken before the Queen's courts for the matter to be resolved.

Before the 12th century the King's peace was enforced locally and personally by the Saxon and early Norman kings. However, other institutions also claimed powers to enforce the peace, particularly the church and some of the great barons. The consequence was that the enforcer of the peace in any locality was the king, cleric or baron – whoever controlled the area.

To ensure that the peace was maintained, courts were needed to administer justice. These courts were not set up entirely out of altruism but for two significant reasons to do with the exploitation of power:

- running courts and administering justice was a profitable undertaking – even then justice was not free;
- ordinary people in a feudal society would be loyal to the lord who provided justice, and this had importance from the point of view of raising military forces.

The King's peace

In the Coronation Charter of Henry I (1101), the King formally claimed the existence of the King's peace. King Henry said that, in effect:

> A disturbance of the peace was not only an offence against the persons aggrieved thereby but was also an affront to the king himself, and the royal power would be deployed against the wrongdoer.

This proclamation was the start of the concept of the King's peace that remains with us to the present time.

Although King Henry claimed the right to maintain a peaceful environment within which men could go about their business undisturbed by violence, the claim was not effective because of the extensive civil unrest of the times. A patchwork of 'peace authorities' existed throughout England until the accession of King Edward I in 1272.

Edward was the most powerful of all of the medieval kings, and probably the greatest of them, having gained his power by force of arms. He used his prerogative power and claimed that he would enforce the King's peace throughout England at all times, To authorise his action he used prerogative powers to enact several major statutes, two of which had a direct bearing on the maintenance of the peace.

The Statute of Winchester

The Statute of Winchester 1285 was enacted to define and enforce 'policing' measures throughout England and it detailed how King Henry's proclaimed peace would be effected. Although this was the first 'Police Act' it embodied many of the things already done in different places under the existing Saxon system of Tithing and the Norman system of Frankpledge. The important features of the Act were:

- citizens were directed to form a 'Hue and Cry' to make a prompt pursuit of criminals from town to town and from county to county;
- the inhabitants of hundreds and franchises would be answerable to the king for any robberies committed within their borders;
- in towns, the town gates were ordered to be closed from sunset to sunrise. Watches had to be kept during the night and bailiffs were required to make inquiries respecting any strangers within the town walls (Watch and Ward);
- in the country, highways had to be widened by the clearance of brushwood for two hundred feet each side of the road to protect travellers from ambush by robbers;
- it was ordered that every free man between the ages of 15 and 60 had to be armed according to his wealth. Alleged defaulters were to be taken before the conservators of the peace who were authorised to punish those guilty. (These conservators of the peace were the forerunners of the present day justices of the peace.)

The Homewatch arrangements that exist in many parts of the country in the 1990s is in part a resurrection of these old concepts of mutual protection although the medieval forms of collective punishment for failure to apprehend offenders is not now acceptable.

Later in the same year, the Statute of Westminster (the second) 1285 was enacted. This statute re-organised the judiciary to ensure that the King controlled the courts thus guaranteeing that the King's peace would be enforceable throughout England to a common standard.

Over five centuries were to elapse before the next major statute affecting national policing followed – this was the Police Act 1829.

The prerogative power to maintain the peace still rests with the crown, although it is not exercised personally by the sovereign. Nowadays the powers are delegated to justices of the peace (note that all judges are *ex officio* justices of the peace), and constables appointed in accordance with the Police Act 1996.

Individual rights

The royal prerogative gives powers to the Crown to enforce the peace with powers that originated in the mists of antiquity. Nowadays, the right of individual citizens not to suffer by the misuse of these powers is considered a matter of importance.

The modern idea of individual rights laid down in law started with the United Nations Universal Declaration of Human Rights. This declaration outlined the rights that individuals ought to have, but provided no practical means of enforcing them.

In 1953 the Council of Europe (note that this Council has no connection with the European Union or Common Market) formulated the Convention for the Protection of Human Rights and Fundamental Freedoms to provide a legal framework in this area. All the Member States of the Council agreed to accept the jurisdiction of the European Court of Human Rights that is located at Strasbourg.

Many of the rights defined in the Convention do not directly concern the police, but the main ones are:

Article 2: The right to life shall be protected by law.

Article 3: Torture or inhuman/degrading treatment is forbidden.

Article 5: The right to liberty and security of person.

Article 6: Entitlement to a fair trial.

Article 7: No one is guilty of a crime unless it is defined in the law.

Article 8: The right to privacy in one's home and correspondence.

Article 9: The right to freedom of expression.

Article 11: The right to freedom of peaceful assembly.

Details of the Convention are in Appendix A.

In England and Wales an individual who believes he has been wronged, can, after he has exhausted all the English court processes, take his case to the Court of Human Rights.

Most of the above rights refer to the methods and procedures used by the police in arresting, detaining, searching and otherwise dealing with alleged offenders. The form of these methods and procedures is legislated for in the Police and Criminal Evidence Act 1984 as amended, and is outside the scope of this handbook.

In some matters, it can be said that the existence of a right could be in conflict with the prerogative power to maintain the peace. Say, for example, a person claimed rights under Articles 9 and 11 and wished to make a contentious speech to a crowd gathered in a public place. The police might fear a breach of the peace would occur as a consequence. In such a case would civil rights or prerogative power be more important?

See the cases of *Duncan v Jones* (1936) on page 12 and *R v Chief Constable of Sussex ex parte ITF Ltd* (1997) on page 59 for examples of this pattern of conflict in practical terms.

Currently (as at 1997) the Human Rights Convention has not been embodied into English law, but there are strong pressures from leading members of the judiciary and senior politicians for this step to be taken. The Convention is not, in consequence, of direct application in the English courts as stated in:

Malone v Metropolitan Police Commissioner (1979)

At Malone's trial it was conceded that his telephone had been tapped and he sought a declaration that his right to privacy under Article 8 had been breached. Sir Robert Megarry VC stated:

> ... Any such right is ... a direct right in relation to the ... European Court of Human Rights and not in relation to the courts of this country, for the Convention is not law here ... the Convention does not, as a matter of English law, confer any direct rights ... that can be enforce(d) in the English courts.

In cases where English statutes have conflicted with the Convention, the English courts have been bound to disregard decisions made by the Court of Human Rights, as:

R v Morrisey (1997)
R v Staines (1997)

It was stated in the Court of Appeal that the English courts had no power to give effect to a judgment of the European Court of Human Rights which would amount to a partial repeal of an English statute.

Their Lordships said that, notwithstanding the fact that the United Kingdom is subject to the treaty obligations giving effect to the European Convention of Human Rights, English courts are not empowered to enforce these rights.

Although, in other cases that have shown no conflict between the Convention and English law, decisions made by the Court of Human Rights have influenced the decisions made by English courts.

Even without the Convention there are a number of both administrative and legal safeguards recognised in English law. They are available to individuals who are victims of either corporate or individual misconduct by police and each of these existing safeguards will be examined separately in this handbook.

It was reported in May 1997 that the Home Secretary is to introduce a statutory Bill of Rights during the next session of Parliament. This Bill will incorporate the European Convention on Human Rights into domestic law thus allowing human rights cases to be heard in British courts instead of the European Court of Human Rights.

A detailed explanation of the new provisions will not be available until the Act reaches the Statute Book and several questions will remain unanswered until that time. For example, how will any legal conflicts between statutory human rights granted to individuals and existing prerogative or statutory powers used to maintain the Queen's peace for the benefit of the community at large be reconciled?

2 **The Office of Constable**

The local character of the police

Policing has always been a local responsibility in England, as shown by the Statute of Winchester 1285. This is in contrast to the national police forces of many other countries. The following description of the local nature of policing is quoted in the report of the Royal Commission on the Police 1962.

> The office of constable in England and Wales is very ancient. It is associated with the village, perhaps the oldest area of local self-government in England. The constable was the executive agent of the village or township, and also its representative. As such, he was required to make quarterly reports known as 'presentments' at courts leet or, after the establishment in the 14th century of justices of the peace, at petty sessions. These reports dealt not only with the arrest of felons and the keeping of the King's peace, but also with the condition of roads and bridges, and many other such matters of purely local administration.

> After Parliament came into being laws were passed requiring constables to make reports on, for example, Popish recusants, persons absenting themselves from their parish church, and profane swearers and cursers. Presentments by constables survived until as late as 1827.

> Thus the constable kept some of his local administrative duties a long time. He also retained, under the supervision of justices, his duties as the local keeper of the peace. Every town and rural parish appointed its constable or constables, and these often appointed deputies of low degree to act for them. In the towns, additional help was given by watchmen, appointed to guard the gates under an ancient system of Watch and Ward authorised by the Statute of Winchester of 1285. Thus no police system as such existed, and law enforcement was a matter for each local community in which all citizens were expected to join in the 'hue and cry' after felons.

> This long tradition of local responsibility for the maintenance of law order was preserved when, in the last century, constables were embodied into the new police forces. It is the persistence of this tradition that helps to explain why there are still so many separate police forces, each identified with its own particular locality.

The local connection of provincial police forces is maintained to the present day and sections 1 and 2 define the 'police areas' for which individual police forces must be maintained. These police areas are coterminous with one or more local council areas in accordance with local needs. A list of police forces is contained in Schedule 1.

Individual provincial police areas can be altered by the Home Secretary by virtue of sections 32, 33 and 34 if:

- he has received a request so to do by the police authorities affected; or
- if it appears expedient to make alterations in the interests of efficiency or effectiveness.

However, before making an order to alter a police area the Home Secretary must consult locally and consider any objections; the form of the consultation is defined in these sections. An important restriction on these alteration orders is that they must not cause a local authority area to be divided between two or more police areas; thus police forces should retain links with specific local authorities.

Police interforce and other co-operation

Although individual police forces have strong local connections, it is obviously necessary for police forces to work in harmony with each other in their task of fighting crime. Following are the main structures of organised co-operation between individual police forces.

Mutual aid between police forces

Mutual aid in some form or other has existed since the formation of modern police forces – big forces frequently helped smaller ones with complex investigations or in dealing with abnormal disorder. However, the first formal authority that allowed forces to make arrangements to help each other came in 1890 and in 1925, following recommendations from the Desborough Committee in 1919, a national mutual aid agreement, covering all police forces in England and Wales was arranged. Since that time any police force in difficulties with major incidents has been able to call upon other forces for assistance by providing either personnel or particular resources.

The chief constable of any police force may, on the application of a chief constable of another police force, provide constables or other assistance for the purpose of enabling the other force to meet any special demand on its resources (section 24). There are like arrangements for mutual aid to and for the National Criminal Intelligence Service (section 23 PA 1997), see page 31.

Similar mutual aid arrangements exist for English and Welsh police forces to assist police forces in Scotland and Northern Ireland (section 98).

If it appears expedient to the Home Secretary, in the interests of public safety or order, that any police force should be reinforced or should receive other assistance for the purpose of enabling it to meet any special demand on its resources and that satisfactory arrangements cannot be made locally, he may direct the chief constable of any police force to provide such constables or other assistance as are required (section 24).

Constables provided for the assistance of another police force, as described above, will act under the direction and control of the receiving chief constable and will, whilst so seconded, have all the powers and privileges of a constable of the receiving force.

The police authority receiving assistance shall pay to the police authority providing assistance such contribution as is agreed between them; in default of such agreement the amount payable will be decided by the Home Secretary. In 1988 the Nottinghamshire and Leicestershire Police Authorities refused to pay a bill for £120,000, part of a £1.1 million claim, made by Thames Valley Police Authority for assistance during the Miners' strike in 1984. The Home Secretary eventually decided the amounts to be paid which were lower than the Thames Valley claim.

Collaboration agreements

If it appears to the chief constables of two or more police forces that any police functions can be more efficiently or effectively discharged by members of those forces acting jointly, they may, with the approval of the police authorities for those areas make an agreement for that purpose. Likewise, if it appears to any two or more police authorities that equipment or other material or facilities can with advantage be provided jointly for their police forces they may make an agreement for that purpose. Underwater Search Units are an example of such collaborative agreements. If the Home Secretary decides that an agreement is required he may direct that such an agreement be made (section 23). There are like arrangements for collaboration agreements between the National Criminal Intelligence Service and other police bodies (section 22 PA 1997), see page 31.

Any expenditure incurred under these agreements will be borne by the police authorities in such proportions as they may agree or in default of agreement be determined by the Home Secretary.

The constable's office and powers

The office and powers of a constable are derived from common law, the first police recognised by statute were the watchmen needed to implement the Watch and Ward system of policing townships in 1285. They might be called the ancestors of today's police officers.

The derivation of a constable's powers was examined by the Royal Commission on Police Powers and Procedures in 1929 who commented as follows:

The police of this country have never been recognised, either in law or by tradition, as a force distinct from the general body of citizens. Despite the imposition of many extraneous duties on the police by legislation or administrative action, the principle remains that a policeman, in the view of the common law, is only **'a person paid to perform, as a matter of duty, acts which if he were so minded he might have done voluntarily'**.

Indeed a policeman possesses few powers not enjoyed by the ordinary citizen, and public opinion, expressed in Parliament and elsewhere, has shown great jealousy of any attempts to give increased authority to the police. This attitude is due, we believe, not to any distrust of the police as a body, but to an instinctive feeling that, as a matter or principle, they should have as few powers as possible which are not possessed by the ordinary citizen, and that their authority should rest on the broad basis of the consent and active co-operation of all law-abiding people. At the same time it must be realised that there are certain duties of a special nature which, if they are to be entrusted to the police and adequately performed by them require the grant of special powers.

It follows that the police, in exercising their functions, are, to a peculiar degree, dependent upon the goodwill of the general public and that the utmost discretion must be exercised by them to avoid over-stepping the limited powers which they possess. A proper and mutual understanding between the police and public is essential for the maintenance of law and order.

The 1962 Commission endorsed the comments adding that whilst police powers are mostly grounded in the common law and differ little from those of ordinary citizens, it is an important corollary that the police can be fully effective only if they enjoy the support of public opinion. The Commission went on to say:

> The same principle, that police power (such as it is) originates in the common law, opens up another field in which we have heard a good deal of evidence, namely, suggestions that because his powers are original and not delegated, the constable therefore enjoys a degree of independence in the exercise of these powers. This claim to a measure of independence from outside control, which is reflected in the terms of the declaration made by a constable on appointment, has far-reaching implications of constitutional significance ...

[Emphasis added by the author. These generalisations ignore the additional powers, especially of arrest, possessed by constables but not by ordinary citizens.]

Attestation of a constable

Section 13 permits the ranks of chief constable, assistant chief constable, superintendent, chief inspector, inspector, sergeant and constable, however, irrespective of their police force rank, all members of a police force are regarded in law as 'constables'.

Every member and every special constable of a police force maintained under the authority of the Police Act shall, on appointment, be attested as a constable by making a declaration before a justice of the peace having jurisdiction within the police area (section 29). The declaration is in the form described in Schedule 4, as follows:

> I, ... of ... do solemnly and sincerely declare and affirm that I will well and truly serve Our Sovereign Lady The Queen in the office of constable, without favour or affection, malice or ill will; and that I will to the best of my power cause the peace to be kept and preserved, and prevent all offences against the persons and properties of Her Majesty's subjects; and that while I continue to hold the said office I will to the best of my skill and knowledge, discharge all the duties thereof faithfully according to law.

Because of the highlighted phrase, each constable, after attestation, when acting as a peace officer, is exercising prerogative power that is devolved to him personally. A constable cannot be ordered to exercise this delegated power as he must believe that there is reasonable cause for its use. In other words a wrongful arrest cannot be defended by a constable claiming to be obeying the orders of a more senior police officer.

Following are two important judicial decisions that have been made in respect of a constable's powers:

Enever v the King (Australia) (1906)

Griffiths CJ said:

> Now the powers of a constable, (who is acting as a) police officer, whether conferred by common law or statute law, are exercised by him by virtue of his office, and cannot be exercised on the responsibility of any person but himself. … A constable therefore, when acting as a peace officer, is not exercising a delegated authority, but an original authority … .

[See also *Fisher v Oldham Corporation* (1930) on page 15.]

R v Chief Constable of Devon and Cornwell ex parte the Central Electricity Generating Board (1981)

Lawton LJ said:

> The (chief constables) commanded their forces but they could not give an officer under command an order to do acts which could only lawfully be done if the officer himself with reasonable cause suspected that a breach of the peace had occurred or was imminently likely to occur or an arrestable offence had been committed.

The Queen's peace is the normal state of society and a breach of that peace is any violation of the quiet, peace and security guaranteed by law for each citizen and constables are empowered to arrest those who breach, or threaten to breach, the peace. When a constable uses this power of arrest he must be satisfied that the actions or threats of the arrested person are likely to harm or put a person in fear (*R v Howell* (1981)). Sometimes this calls for the arrest of a person based upon suspected future events, in other words the action may be either preventative or reactive.

Statutory support for a constable's prerogative power

The Prevention of Crime Act 1871 created the summary offence of assaulting a constable in the execution of his duty and the Prevention of Crime Amendment Act 1885 created the summary offences of resisting or wilfully obstructing a constable in the execution of his duty. These offences were subsequently included in later Police Acts and are now enacted as:

Section 89

1 Any person who assaults a constable in the execution of his duty, or a person assisting a constable in the execution of his duty shall be guilty of an offence.

2 Any person who resists or wilfully obstructs a constable in the execution of his duty, or a person assisting a constable in the execution of his duty, shall be guilty of an offence.

There are a number of cases that have defined these powers over the course of the years. The first case cited, *Humphries*, occurred before obstructing a constable became a specific offence.

Humphries v Conor (1864)

An action against a police officer for assault, as he had gently removed an orange lily from the plaintiff in an Irish town, failed, as the officer was authorised to do everything necessary and proper to remove a provocation which might cause a breach of the peace. The plaintiff had caused a large and threatening crowd to gather in this case.

The leading case in this aspect of law is that of *Duncan*. The decision is still a matter of contention among jurists.

Duncan v Jones (1936)

The events leading to this case involved a Mrs Duncan who had been about to make a speech in the street opposite a training centre for the unemployed. There had been a disturbance in the training centre following an earlier meeting which she had addressed.

A police inspector told her that the meeting had to be held in a street about 175 yards away but Mrs Duncan refused to move and persisted in trying to hold the meeting. In consequence she was arrested, charged and convicted of obstructing a police officer in the execution of his duty.

At Quarter Sessions the justices found that:

- Mrs Duncan must have known of the probable consequence of the meeting at that spot, a disturbance as before, and a possible breach of the peace, and she was not unwilling that such consequences should ensue.
- Inspector Jones reasonably apprehended a breach of the peace.
- His duty was, therefore, to prevent the holding of the meeting.
- By attempting to hold the meeting Mrs Duncan obstructed the Inspector in the execution of his duty.

The prosecution made no allegation that either the highway had been obstructed or that Mrs Duncan had committed, incited or provoked a breach of the peace, therefore her conduct was apparently lawful until she disobeyed inspector Jones' instruction to move the meeting to a new position.

Mrs Duncan appealed by way of case stated but her appeal was rejected and Humphreys, J said:

It does not require authority to emphasise the statement that it is the duty of a police officer to prevent apprehended breaches of the peace. It then … becomes his duty to prevent anything which in his view would cause that breach of the peace.

The *Duncan* case has been criticised on the grounds that it appears to weight the balance more heavily than is desirable in favour of public order as perceived by the police. It is claimed by some that Mrs Duncan was convicted merely because she disobeyed a policeman as no other offences were proven against her.

More recent cases in this area are:

Piddington v Bates (1960)

Lord Parker, CJ, said:

> I think that a police officer charged with the duty of preserving the Queen's Peace must be left to take such steps as, on the evidence before him, he thinks proper.

Rice v Connolly (1966)

To 'obstruct' is to do any act which makes it more difficult for the police to carry out their duty. Apart from a few special cases, there is no legal obligation on citizens to help police in their inquiries. However, when questions are answered the answers must be truthful because telling lies amounts to obstruction.

Wershof v Commissioner of the Police of the Metropolis (1978)

At common law a police officer has power to arrest without warrant a person who wilfully obstructs him in the execution of his duty, but only if:

- The nature of the obstruction was such that the offender actually caused or was likely to cause a breach of the peace or was calculated to prevent the lawful arrest or detention of another person; or
- At the relevant time the police officer was acting in the execution of his duty and honestly believed on reasonable grounds that the offender was wilfully obstructing him and that the obstruction was likely to cause a breach of the peace.

R v Howell (1981)

In addition to the power to arrest an offender for an actual breach of the peace or the threat of its renewal, constables have a power of arrest without warrant where they honestly and reasonably believe that a breach of the peace is in imminent danger of being committed.

R v the Chief Constable of Devon and Cornwall ex parte the Central Electricity Generating Board (1981)

Lord Denning said:

> ... in deciding whether there is a breach of the peace or the apprehension of it, the law does not go into the rights or wrongs of the matter ... Suffice it that the peace is broken or likely to be broken ... with the result that ... any police officer can intervene to stop the breaches.

Moss and others v Charles McLachlan (1984)

During the miners' strike of 1984–85 Moss and others were driving cars towards collieries, about two to five miles distant, at which a mass picket was forming. Police stopped the cars, told the occupants that they believed a breach of the peace would ensue if they continued. Further, if they tried to continue they would be obstructing a police officer in the execution of his duty. Appellants attempted to continue, were arrested, charged and convicted.

The appeal was dismissed, and it was held that on the justices' findings of fact, anyone with knowledge of the current strike would realise that there was a substantial risk of an outbreak of violence. The mere presence of such a body of men at the junction in question in the context of the current situation in the Nottinghamshire coalfields would have been enough to justify the police in taking preventive action.

The possibility of a breach of the peace must be real to justify any preventive action. The imminence or immediacy of the threat to the peace determined what action was reasonable.

Lewis and another v the Chief Constable of Greater Manchester (1991)

A police officer has the power of arrest for a breach of the peace although a breach of the peace has not yet occurred, provided he honestly believes on reasonable grounds that a breach of the peace is about to take place.

In addition to the above powers, a constable is vested with other powers to arrest, search people and places and seize property that are authorised by other laws. Examples of such authorities are:

- common law;
- Criminal Law Act 1967;
- Police and Criminal Evidence Act 1984; and
- particular statutes giving specific powers to constables.

The constable is not above the law and if the powers are improperly used then he may be prosecuted or sued in the Royal Courts of Justice according to the general principles of criminal and/or civil liability.

As the powers of a constable are very wide ranging, the law takes a serious view of their fraudulent use by any unauthorised person and particular offences exist to deal with such people.

Section 90

It is an offence for any person who with intent to deceive impersonates a member of a police force or special constable, or do any act calculated falsely to suggest that he is such a member or constable.

It is also an offence for anyone who is not a constable, to wear any article of police uniform in circumstances where he resembles a constable or to possess any article of police uniform without lawful authority.

Jurisdiction of a constable

Constables in the police forces that were formed after 1829 had, in general terms, jurisdiction in their own force area and in those areas immediately adjacent. Since then the jurisdiction of constables in English and Welsh police forces has been expanded and is now detailed in section 30 as follows:

A member of a police force has all the powers and privileges of a constable throughout England and Wales and the adjacent United Kingdom waters.

A special constable shall have all the powers and privileges of a constable in the police area for which he is appointed and, where the boundary of that area includes the coast, in the adjacent United Kingdom waters, and in any other police area that is contiguous to his own police area.

Jurisdiction was extended by the Criminal Justice and Public Order Act 1994 to include the following power:

> Any constable of a police force in England and Wales who has reasonable grounds for suspecting that an arrestable offence has been committed or attempted in England or Wales and that the suspected person is in Scotland or in Northern Ireland may arrest without warrant the suspected person wherever he is in Scotland or Northern Ireland.

Procedural details in respect of how the prisoner is dealt with are contained in sections 137–40 of the 1994 Act.

Status of a constable

A constable in a provincial police force is appointed by the local police authority but he exercises Crown authority when performing his duty. The dichotomy between accountability to both Crown and local authority makes it difficult to specify the exact status of a constable, as he is neither a Crown servant nor a local authority employee.

In a number of leading cases some particular points of this confusing status have been examined.

Mackalley's case (1611)

The constable's oath and his close relationship with the justices of the peace characterised him as a ministerial officer of the Crown like a sheriff or the justices of the peace rather than a mere local administrative officer.

The next case, the *Fisher* judgment is probably the most important definition of a constable's status in the eyes of the law. Many later cases refer to it as the authoritative precedent.

Fisher v Oldham Corporation (1930)

In this case the plaintiff Fisher claimed damages in a civil action against the Borough of Oldham for false imprisonment by a constable appointed by Oldham Watch Committee. McCardie J, cited, with approval, the judgment in *Enever v the King* and that the police authority had no power to control the constable's execution of the duties of his office, since the relation between master and servant did not exist between it and the police. The police fulfilled their duties as public servants and officers of the Crown, sworn to preserve the peace. He said:

> ... a police constable is not the servant of the [local police authority], he is a servant of the state, a ministerial officer of the central power, though subject, in some respects, to local supervision and local regulation.

It was also said, *obiter dicta*, that if a police authority passed a resolution instructing the police to release a man arrested for a serious offence then they would not only be under a plain duty to disregard the resolution but would also be under a duty to consider 'whether an information should not at once be laid against the [authority] for a conspiracy to obstruct the course of criminal justice'.

It was held that Oldham Corporation could not be held to be vicariously liable for the tortious acts of a constable; he, the constable, was personally liable in law.

Attorney General for New South Wales v Perpetual Trustee Co (1955)

Viscount Simonds approved both the Enever and Fisher judgments and he said:

> ... neither changes in organisation nor the imposition of ever-increasing statutory duties have altered the fundamental character of the constable's office. Today, as in the past, he is in common parlance described in terms which aptly define his legal position as 'a police officer', 'an officer of justice', an 'officer of the peace'.

Ridge v Baldwin (1964)

In this case the lack of an ordinary contractual relationship between Chief Constable Ridge and the Police Authority was an important element in deciding whether Ridge was an employee or the holder of a public office. It was held that he was a public officer.

A special case relating to public security is:

Lewis v Cattle (1938)

A constable was held to be **a person holding office under His Majesty for the purpose of the Official Secrets Acts**, thus, he is subject to the terms of those Acts.

The constable, however, is not paid out of the Consolidated Fund, and, outside the metropolitan area, he is not appointed directly or indirectly by the Crown. A police constable does not satisfy, therefore, the requirements of what constitutes a Crown servant specified in section 2(6) Crown Proceedings Act 1947.

Status for health and safety at work purposes

Another special case pertains to occupational health and safety laws. For this purpose a constable is regarded as an employee of the chief constable (section 1 Police (Health and Safety) Act 1997).

For constables seconded to either the National Criminal Intelligence Service or the National Crime Squad, the employer is presumed to be the appropriate Director General.

Constables and members of trade unions

On four occasions police officers have withdrawn their labour in England and Wales. Each strike was brought about as a result of poor pay and conditions relative to other contemporary workers. The first two strikes, referred to as 'mutinies' at the time, occurred in 1872 and 1890, being confined to particular Divisions of the Metropolitan Police.

Before and during the Great War (1914–18), many Metropolitan police officers together with members of provincial City and Borough Forces joined the National Union of Police and Prison Officers (NUPPO). The reason was that during the war pay deteriorated relatively as, unlike other workers who had their pay increased in line with inflation, the police continued to receive about the same wage. Additionally, other working conditions had also deteriorated leading to wide-scale resentment.

The Union called its first strike in August 1918 and it took place at the same time as severe fighting was taking place on the Western Front. Only members of the Metropolitan Police were involved and their representatives attended a meeting with Prime Minister Lloyd George to settle the strike. The policemen were given to understand that steps would be taken to improve conditions and to give official recognition to NUPPO. After 44 hours the strike finished with police officers cheering Lloyd George and the resignation of the unpopular Commissioner of Police.

The War finished in November 1918 and NUPPO then pressed for the implementation of the promised improvements. The government responded by setting up a Committee of Inquiry under Lord Desborough to examine conditions in the police service. The Committee reported on 14 July 1919 and recommended increased pay rates, a plan for a representative body for the police and banning of trade union membership.

NUPPO was aggrieved and referred to the 1918 agreement, but Lloyd George denied that he had ever made an agreement to recognise the trade union, and on the basis of the Desborough Report, a new Police Bill was introduced into Parliament embodying the recommendations. NUPPO called for a national strike to seek official recognition, scheduled to start on 31 July 1919 (August Bank Holiday weekend).

The trade union was outmanoeuvred by Prime Minister Lloyd George who shrewdly increased police pay, back-dating the increase to the previous April with payment at the new rate taking effect immediately.

The strike started over the weekend in London, Liverpool, Bootle and Birkenhead with lesser support in Wallasey and Birmingham. There was never full support for the strike merely to achieve union recognition, not even in Merseyside, and it petered out by 4 August 1919. However, there was severe rioting in Merseyside which resulted in the deployment of armed troops and the sending of warships to the Mersey to regain order.

The Police Bill was passed into law in 1919, and the relevant sections are now continued in the current Police Act.

Section 91 makes it an offence to cause disaffection amongst the members of any police force, or to induce any member of a police force to withhold his services.

There are similar offences of causing disaffection amongst members of the National Criminal Intelligence Service and the National Crime Squad under sections 43 and 87 Police Act 1997.

Section 64 states that a member of a police force shall not be a member of any trade union having for its objects, or one of its objects, to control or influence pay, pensions or conditions of service of any police force. This regulation also applies to police cadets.

A member of a police force who was a member of a trade union when he became a member of a police force, may, with the approval of the chief constable, continue such membership during his service.

Police Federation (section 59)

The 1919 Act also set up the Police Federation designed to represent the interests of members of police forces. The purpose of the body is to represent members in all matters affecting their welfare and efficiency except for questions of promotion or discipline affecting individuals. Members holding the ranks of constable to chief inspector are referred to as 'federated ranks' being directly represented by the Police Federation. Officers of the rank of Superintendent are members of the Superintendents' Association and chief officers are members of the Association of Chief Police Officers for similar representation.

The Home Secretary is authorised to control the constitution and governing regulations for Federation proceedings, funding, how representations may be made and payment of expenses incurred in Federation business (section 60).

R v Chief Constable of North Wales ex parte Hughes (1990)

The Court of Appeal decided that a police officer who had been suspended did not automatically cease to be a member of the Police Federation, but a chief constable could lawfully order a suspended officer not to attend federation meetings where there was evidence of a substantial risk to the reputation and working of the force.

Note that a suspended police officer is barred from acting as a constable although he remains a member of his police force for the purposes of discipline.

Health and safety representatives

For the purpose of appointing safety representatives under the Health and Safety at Work Act 1974 the Police Federation is treated as the 'recognised trade union' in respect of members of police forces (section 1 of the Police (Health and Safety) Act 1997).

Police Negotiating Board (section 61)

This Board consists a chairman appointed by the Prime Minister and representatives of:

- police authorities;
- members of police forces;
- Commissioner of the Metropolitan Police;
- Home Secretary.

Its duty is to consider questions relating to hours of duty, leave, pay and allowances, pensions and the issue, use or return of clothing equipment and accoutrements.

The Home Secretary must consider any recommendations made by the Board before making any police regulations in respect of matters considered by the Board (section 62).

Police Advisory Board (section 63)

This Board is intended to advise the Home Secretary on general questions relating to police matters.

The constitution and proceedings are decided by the Home Secretary after consulting representatives of police authorities and members of police forces. The Board should be shown drafts of any proposed police regulations, and the Home Secretary must take into consideration any representations made by the Board.

The duties of a constable

The duties of the 'new police' in 1829 were defined in the instruction book written by Commissioners Rowan and Mayne for distribution to the recruits. Amongst other things it says:

> It should be understood, at the outset, that the principal object to be attained is the Prevention of Crime. To this great end every effort of the Police is to be directed. The security of person and property, the preservation of the public tranquillity, and all the other objects of a Police Establishment, will thus be better effected, than by the detection and punishment of the offender, after he has succeeded in committing the crime. This should constantly be kept in mind by every member of the Police Force, as the guide for his own conduct. Officers and Police Constables should endeavour to distinguish themselves by such vigilance and activity, as may render it extremely difficult for any one to commit a crime within that portion of the town under their charge.

The Royal Commission on the Police 1962 in reviewing the status and duties of the police commented as follows:

> The policeman works in a changing society, and there is nothing constant about the range and variety of police duties, just as there is nothing constant about the pattern of crime, the behaviour of criminals, the state of public order or, at deeper levels, the hidden trends in society that dispose men to crime, to civil and industrial unrest, or to political demonstration. The emphasis on particular duties varies from one generation to another. At present, however, the main functions of the police may be summarised as follows:
>
> 1 The police have a duty to maintain law and order and to protect persons and property.
>
> 2 They have a duty to prevent crime.
>
> 3 They are responsible for the detection of criminals, and in the course of interrogating suspected persons, they have a part to play in the early stages of the judicial process, acting under judicial restraint.
>
> 4 The police in England and Wales have the responsibility of deciding whether or not to prosecute persons suspected of criminal offences. [Now the responsibility of the Crown Prosecution Service.]
>
> 5 In England and Wales the police themselves conduct many prosecutions for the less serious offences. [Now the responsibility of the Crown Prosecution Service.]

6 The police have the duty of controlling road traffic and advising local authorities on traffic questions.

7 The police carry out certain duties on behalf of government departments, for example, they conduct enquiries into applications made by persons who wish to be granted British nationality.

8 They have by long tradition a duty to befriend anyone who needs their help, and they may at any time be called upon to cope with minor or major emergencies.

There is no legal definition, either by law or by judicial decision that gives an all embracing definition of a constable's duties although two cases have examined very limited areas of those duties:

R v Chief Constable of Gwent Constablulary ex parte Champion (1989)

The House of Lords decided that for a police officer to serve on a school appointments committee, which interviewed and recommended candidates for teaching posts, was not an activity likely to give rise amongst members of the public that it might interfere with the impartial discharge of his police duties.

R v Chief Constable of Cheshire Constabulary ex parte Kirwan (1989)

The police are not under any duty to intervene or assist in enforcing a custody order under the Guardianship of Minors Act 1971, or a mother's rights under section 85(7) Children's Act 1975, unless it was clear that a threat of danger to the child or a breach of the peace was imminent.

Recent matters concerning the duties of a constable

During the 1980s, following the large-scale disorders of 1981 and the miners' strike in 1984, there was much public and political discussion about the duties and accountability of the police. As a result several public and privately inspired reports were written to try and provide a 'bobby's job description' but a major difficulty was met when trying to define what was and was not a police duty.

In 1994 the Police and Magistrates' Courts Act 1994 gave the Home Secretary power to set policing objectives and performance targets. This power is now contained in the Police Act 1996 (see page 75). Although this was not a 'job description', it did mean that the work of the police could be measured to assess efficiency.

Also in 1994 the Home Secretary instigated a review of what he called the 'core functions' of the police. The review team surveyed four main areas of police tasks and in 1995 submitted a report titled Review of Core and Ancillary Tasks. The following comments are abstracted from the report:

1 To protect, help and reassure the community

... from the earliest days the police remit ran wider than crime fighting and law enforcement. The public looked to the police to deal with any threat to their safety or tranquillity. Sometimes the threat arose directly from an actual or potential criminal act or disorderly behaviour. Just as often the call for help related to a general anxiety about safety in which illegality played little part.

The principle of the omni-competent constable envisaged in the earliest days of professional policing has proved enduring. In many countries a separate quasi-military police has specialised in public order. In this country, the officer who walks the beat or drives the patrol car is also trained to deal with riots.

It has often proved difficult to live up to this rather idealised concept of police officer as both strong authority figure and ever ready friend. Those sections of the community who regularly run foul of the law may not always construe more, or more highly visible policing, as friendly.

2 To uphold the law

The state has no more basic function than ensuring the safety and security of it citizens. In a civil society this requires an adequate and acceptable means of upholding and enforcing the law, so that citizens can enjoy 'the Queen's peace'.

The police service is the body primarily entrusted by the state to carry out this function when citizens fail individually or collectively to behave peacefully and lawfully. To that end they are given a range of extraordinary powers beyond those accorded to the ordinary citizen and are vested with the right to exercise legitimate force where it is required to uphold the law or maintain the peace.

The role of the police in upholding the law is symbolic as well as actual. The existence of a police to which all citizens have access on a basis of need reinforces the public's belief that they live in an orderly society and partly accounts for the consistent demand for a more visible police presence. Through this visible representation of authority, the police effectively uphold the law when undertaking many tasks which do not directly address breaches of the law or conflict resolution. When disorder does occur, knowledge that the police have been called is often sufficient to resolve a conflict before their arrival on the scene.

3 To bring to justice those who break the law

... Historically the police were responsible for both [the investigation and prosecution of crime] ... [but since 1985] the responsibility for prosecutions [has been] placed in the hands of the independent Crown Prosecution Service, although leaving the police with the initial decision as to whether or not to initiate proceedings by charging an offender.

In May 1993 the Home Secretary, concerned about evidence of the high level of paperwork following an arrest, commissioned a consultancy with a view to reducing administrative burdens. [The findings are being taken forward with a view to implementation.]

4 To fight and prevent crime

The police recognised the need for change to cope with the burgeoning workload and to try to stem the growth in crime. They perceived the limitations of the prevalent crime control techniques of patrol, fast response and retrospective investigation of crime. Untargeted patrolling officers seldom encountered criminals at work, fast response can rarely catch an offender red-handed as the majority of calls are made well after the criminal has left the scene. In the absence of witnesses willing and able to identify the culprit, retrospective investigation is time-consuming and has a limited success rate.

This has resulted in the gradual introduction of a more strategic approach to the fight against crime. Traditional methods have been augmented with a proactive, intelligence based crime management model and a move towards more community based and problem solving approaches to tackling crime.

The report made 26 recommendations to remove or reduce police involvement in peripheral tasks that police at present undertake but concluded that there was little scope for the police service to withdraw completely from large areas of current police work.

This report seems to infer that the review of the Royal Commission on the Police 1962 of the status and duties of the police must still hold good in principle.

The 1995 report was followed by an Audit Commission report, 'Streetwise: Effective Police Patrol', published in 1996. This report did not so much try to define the constable's duties, as look at the way they were performed, the object being to improve efficiency. This report describes a uniformed constable on patrol as the principal means by which the police:

- respond appropriately to crimes, other incidents and emergencies;
- maintain public order and tackle anti-social behaviour;
- reassure the public through a visible police presence;
- forge links with local communities to reduce problems of crime and nuisance;
- gather intelligence, especially in relation to crime and criminals.

The report goes on to say:

The first two types of patrol activity can loosely be described as reactive, in that they are driven primarily by incidents, while the other three are more proactive. Partly because of this range of key activities, there has until recently been no agreed definition of patrol nor, more importantly, consensus about what it is meant to achieve. In fact, there has long been debate as to whether patrol is a task in itself, or a tool to achieve specific objectives.

The other reason why a definition is hard to pin down is the complex and interrelated nature of patrol work – it cannot readily be split into discrete tasks and then assigned to different officers. For example, the single act of arresting someone committing a serious public nuisance could fulfil all five of these objectives at once. An officer on patrol may, while on an apparently routine patrol of the high street, be first on the scene of a fatal accident, or apprehend a street robber.

The second paragraph above sums up the difficulties inherent in trying to devise a 'bobby's job description' in the conventional terms of other occupations because the public expect him to be able to cope with any problem that is presented to him, whether it be knowing the time or saving life. This is perhaps, another factor in the uniqueness of the status and role of the constable.

Abuse of status by a constable

Constables are answerable to the law if their actions are deemed to be an abuse of their status.

R v Browning (1975)

A police officer abuses his status if, during the course of his duty he uses his status to steal even a small sum and will face a custodial sentence. This principle does not apply if the offence had no connection with the police officer's work.

Misconduct in a public office by a constable

An indictment lies at common law against a public officer (which includes a constable) for neglecting the duties required of him by common law or by statute. If a statute requires him to do what, without the statute, has been his duty, it is not imposing a new duty, and he is indictable at common law for the neglect. The element of culpability required is not restricted to corruption or dishonesty, although it has to be such that the conduct impugned was calculated to injure the public interest and calls for condemnation and punishment.

The offence was first defined many years ago as follows:

Crouther's case (1600)

It was held that a constable may be indicted for refusing, on notice, to pursue a felon.

R v Pinney (1832)

This was a case brought against the mayor of Bristol following his failure to fulfil his common law duty to take action during the widespread riots of 1831. Littledale, J, stated the law to be as follows:

... every person entrusted with the duty of putting down a riot, whether by virtue of an office of his own seeking as in the ordinary case of a magistrate, or imposed upon him as in that of a constable, was bound to hit the exact line between excess and failure of duty, and that the difficulty of so doing, though it might be ground for a lenient consideration of his conduct on the part of the jury, was no legal defence to a charge of failing to perform his duty.

A more recent case was:

R v Dytham (1979)

Dytham, a uniformed constable was about 30 yards away from a club entrance when a man was ejected and then noisily kicked to death in the gutter. Dytham made no move to intervene, no attempt to quell the disturbance or stop the attack upon the victim.

He was charged with misconduct of an officer of justice in that, being present and a witness to a criminal offence of violent assault, he deliberately failed to carry out his duty as a police constable by wilfully omitting to take any steps to preserve the Queen's peace or to protect the person of the victim or otherwise to bring to justice his assailants. He was convicted and his appeal was rejected.

Following the Hillsborough disaster in 1989 there was a suggestion in the press that one or more of the senior officers involved in the incident would be charged with this offence, but no such action was taken.

In 1990 it was alleged that two police officers had remained in a police car at Chudleigh in Devon when three other officers were severely assaulted. The Deputy Chief Constable of Devon and Cornwall subsequently stated that the Director of Public Prosecutions had decided that there was insufficient evidence to justify any prosecution. A corollary to this report came to notice when two constables lost a High Court libel action against *The People* newspaper. They were accused of cowardice, failing to help colleagues under attack by a crowd at Chudleigh and, subsequently lying about the incident.

Misfeasance in a public office

Misfeasance means the improper performance of an act that is lawful in itself. Misfeasance in a public office is a civil tort that can be instituted against an individual police officer. The tort is described in the following case:

Racz v Home Office (1992)

In the Court of Appeal Lord Neill declared that the deliberate abuse of power by a person holding a public office was tortious. In order to establish an actionable tort it was necessary to prove either:

1 that the officer or authority knew that it did not possess the power to take the action in question; or

2 that the officer or authority was actuated by malice, for example, by personal spite or a desire to injure for improper reasons.

Lord Neill also quoted from *Weldon v Home Office* (1992) in which Lord Bridge said:

A prison officer who acted in bad faith by subjecting a prisoner to a restraint which he knew he had no authority to impose might render himself personally liable for the tort of misfeasance in public office ...

This case subsequently went to the House of Lords where the question of vicarious liability was examined (see pages 128 and 143).

Elliott v Chief Constable of Wiltshire and others (1996)

Police officers have a status that is the source of important powers and duties. If they are guilty of misconduct and the ingredients of malice, intent to injure, improper purpose and damage are present, misfeasance in a public office is made out.

See also page 139 *et seq* for more details of this and other torts.

Misuse of police computer data

Following the introduction of computers to process police records, concerns have been raised about the security of such sensitive material. Since 1981 there have been statements by journalists about supposed police improprieties in these matters. Most of the early allegations centred on inappropriate and defective security measures rather than corrupt practices by police officers and as a result access to both the Police National Computer (PNC) and other local computers became more stringently controlled.

However, there have been some cases of police officers making improper use of computers holding sensitive data. Following are some examples reported in the press.

In 1986 a Metropolitan Police detective constable was charged under the Official Secrets Act (see *Lewis v Cattle* (1938) re use of this Act). He had allegedly obtained details of men with homosexual convictions for improper use (*Daily Mail*, 13 December 1986).

In 1987 a special constable's personal computer was found to have data taken from the PNC together with details about fellow police officers. He was charged under the Data Protection Act (*The Independent*, 24 October 1997).

In 1996 a police superintendent allegedly breached the Act but the Crown Prosecution Service declined to prosecute. In the event, following disciplinary proceedings the superintendent was required to resign from his force (*Police Review*, 22 November 1996).

Most recently, after a three year investigation, four former officers of Leicestershire Constabulary were prosecuted for offences of conspiracy to pervert the course of justice and conspiracy to gain illegal access to the PNC. The circumstances were that two of the officers, after leaving the force, set up private detective agencies. Two other, still serving, officers used their positions to gain information from police computers that was passed on to the private detective agencies. All four defendants were convicted (*Police Review*, 28 March 1997).

Racial discrimination by a constable on duty

The following decision makes it clear that individual constables are under a duty to act without discrimination when performing their duty as a constable.

The case also emphasises that a constable is personally answerable for any unlawful discrimination that he might engage in.

Farah v Commissioner of Police of the Metropolis (1996)

Farah, a 17 year old Somali girl was attacked by white teenagers who set a dog on to her. A 999 call brought police to the scene, but instead of helping her and seeking to detain her attackers, arrested her without cause. She was charged with affray, common assault and causing unnecessary suffering to a dog. No evidence was offered when she appeared to answer the charges and she was acquitted.

Subsequently she brought a civil action when it was held that police officers were subject to the Race Relations Act 1976 and it was unlawful for them to discriminate in the provision of services, including the provision of protection from crime.

See also page 127 for further details in respect of the vicarious liability of a chief constable in civil litigation.

Special constables

The chief constable may appoint special constables and all special constables for a police area shall be under the direction and control of, and subject to dismissal, by the chief constable (section 27).

Jurisdiction of special constables (section 30)

A special constable shall have all the powers and privileges of a constable in the police area for which he is appointed and where the boundary of that area includes the coast, in the adjacent United Kingdom waters and in any police area which is contiguous to his own police area.

A special constable who is for the time being required to serve in another police force has the same powers and privileges of a special constable appointed to that force.

The status of a special constable was judicially examined in the following case (the details of the present Police Act are the same as those in the 1964 Act):

Sheikh v Anderton (1989)

By the Police Act 1964 a member of a police force has all the powers and privileges of a constable, and a special constable has all the powers and privileges of a constable in the police area for which he is appointed and as far as this goes the powers and privileges are the same for both regular and special constables.

Police cadets

The chief constable may, in accordance with regulations, appoint persons as police cadets to undergo training with a view to becoming members of the police force. All police cadets shall be under the control of, and subject to dismissal by the chief constable (section 28).

Police cadets – employer

The police authority shall, for the purposes of any enactment relating to the functions of employers and of any rule of law with respect to the vicarious liability of employers, be treated as the employer of any police cadets undergoing training with a police force.

However, for the purpose of health and safety at work legislation a police cadet is considered to be the employee of his chief constable (section 1 of the Police (Health and Safety) Act 1997).

Wiltshire Police Authority v Wynn (1980)

A police cadet is being taught and is not doing work as a constable, nor employed as such. A police cadet is not under a contract of service and is not in consequence an employee under the terms of employment law. A complaint of unfair dismissal cannot be sustained.

Like members of the police force, cadets are not permitted to belong to a trade union without the permission of the chief constable (section 64), see page 17.

Civilian employees

A police authority may employ persons to assist the police force maintained by it or to enable it to discharge its functions. Civilian employees are under the direction and control of the chief constable, who also has the powers of appointment and dismissal (section 15).

All civilian employees, unlike constables, are entitled to belong to an independent trade union and they cannot be dismissed or disciplined solely for either being a member of a trade union, or for not being a member of a trade union (Trade Union and Labour Relations (Consolidation) Act 1992).

Misconduct in a public office

Civilian employees as well as constables have a duty towards the public that they must perform in accordance with the law.

R v Bowden (1995)

The Court of Appeal held that the common law offence of misconduct in a public office applies to every person who is compensated from public funds for discharging a public duty. No distinction is made between officers of the Crown or local authorities for this purpose.

3 National and International Police Institutions

General

All police forces in England and Wales are associated with some national and international organisations, important institutions relating to provincial police forces are shown below.

National services

The Police Act 1997 gives legal form to two national police organisations – the National Criminal Intelligence Service (NCIS) and the National Crime Squad (NCS). The two organisations have similar structures, see Chapter 7 for details of their controlling authorities.

Personnel of national services

The personnel consist of (sections 9 and 55 PA 1997):
- a Director General;
- police members;
- other persons appointed as employees by the Service Authority.

Police members must be:
- persons appointed to the rank of assistant chief constable in NCIS/NCS (they must already hold that rank, the rank of commander or higher in the metropolitan police or be eligible for appointment to those ranks); or
- serving members of a police force seconded for temporary service with NCIS/ NCS in accordance with section 97, see page 32.

The Director General

The Directors General direct and control the NCIS/NCS (sections 10 and 56 PA 1997) and hold the police rank of chief constable.

The appointment of the Director General follows the same principles as the appointment of the chief constable of a provincial police force (sections 6 and 52 PA 1997) and there is a similar overview by the Home Secretary, including the right to call for his retirement in the interests of efficiency or effectiveness (sections 7 and 53 PA 1997).

The Director General, after consultation with the Service Authority, will designate a deputy to act during his absence or if there is a vacancy in his office. The deputy may only act as such for three months unless the consent of the Home Secretary has been obtained (sections 8 and 54 PA 1997).

Consultation with other organisations

The Directors General, after consulting their National Authority, must make arrangements for obtaining views about their own organisation (sections 41 and 85 PA 1997). The following will be consulted:

- the chief officers of police of all police forces in England and Wales, Scotland and Northern Ireland;
- the Director General of the NCIS/NCS as appropriate;
- the Commissioners of Customs and Excise; and
- any other persons considered to be appropriate.

Reports

At the end of each financial year the Director General must submit to his Service Authority a general report on the activities of NCIS/NCS during that year (sections 11 and 57 PA 1997). These reports must also be published in an appropriate manner.

A National Service Authority may require their Director General to submit a report on specified matters connected with the activities of NCIS/NCS (sections 11 and 57 PA 1997). If it appears to the Director General that such a report would contain information which in the public interest ought not to be disclosed, or is not needed for the discharge of the functions of the Authority, he may request the Authority to refer the requirement to the Home Secretary. In such cases the requirement shall be of no effect unless it is confirmed by the Home Secretary. The Authority may arrange for a required report to be published in an appropriate manner.

Service plan

The Directors General must each prepare a draft service plan to be submitted to their respective Authority (sections 4 and 50 PA 1997). This plan will show the proposed arrangements for carrying out NCIS/NCS functions during the year and will include:

- a statement of the priorities for the year ahead;
- the financial resources expected to be available;
- the proposed allocation of those resources;
- particulars of
  - any objectives determined by the Home Secretary;
  - any objectives determined by the Service Authority; and
  - any performance targets established by the Service Authority.

After the Service Authority has approved the service plan the Director General must always pay due regard to it when carrying out his functions.

National Criminal Intelligence Service (NCIS)

The functions of the NCIS

The functions of the NCIS are to (section 2 PA 1997):

- gather, store and analyse information in order to provide criminal intelligence;

- provide criminal intelligence to police forces in Great Britain, the Royal Ulster Constabulary, the National Crime Squad and other law enforcement agencies;
- act in support of such organisations in carrying out their criminal intelligence activities.

The Director General is the designated person responsible for co-ordinating police and Security Service Activities in the context of section 2 of the Security Service Act 1989 (section 12 PA 1997), see pages 38–39.

Special services

The Director General of NCIS may, at the request of any person, provide services at any premises or in any locality in the United Kingdom, if those services are consistent with the functions of, and do not prejudice the efficiency or effectiveness of, NCIS (section 24 PA 1997).

Mutual aid

Mutual aid arrangements may be made between the NCIS and other police forces including the NCS (section 23 PA 1997).

Collaboration agreements

The NCIS may enter into collaboration agreements with any other police force in England, Wales, Scotland or Northern Ireland, or with the National Crime Squad in a similar manner as other police forces, see page 9 (section 22 PA 1997).

National Crime Squad (NCS)

The functions of the NCS

The functions of the NCS are to (section 48 PA 1997):

- prevent and detect serious crime which is of relevance to more than one police area in England and Wales.

The Squad may also:

- at the request of a chief constable act in support of the activities of his force in the prevention and detection of serious crime;
- at the request of the Director General of NCIS act in support of NCIS;
- institute criminal proceedings;
- co-operate with other police forces in UK in the prevention and detection of serious crime;
- act in support of other law enforcement agencies in the prevention and detection of serious crime.

Police Information Technology Organisation (PITO)

PITO is a statutory body founded by section 109 and Schedule 8 Police Act 1997. The purpose of PITO is to:

carry out activities, including the commissioning of research, relating to information technology equipment and systems for the use of the police.

Information technology is defined as including any computer or other technology by means of which information or other matter may be recorded or communicated without being reduced to documentary form.

Other police common services

The Home Secretary may provide and maintain any organisations, facilities and services as he considers necessary to promote the efficiency and effectiveness of the police. All police forces in England and Wales can be required to use certain specified facilities or services (such as the arrangements for initial training) if it is considered desirable to do so (section 57).

The Home Secretary can also set up bodies for the purpose of undertaking research into matters affecting the efficiency or effectiveness of the police (section 58).

Some services, such as the Forensic Science Service since 1991, are now provided on an agency basis and it now aims to recover its full costs through making direct charges on its customers.

The Police National Network (PNN) provides a modern telecommunications link for all forces in England and Wales and this service is provided by a private sector supplier who will levy charges on forces.

It seems probable that other services will be provided in a similar manner in the future.

Seconded police officers

Police officers seconded for temporary service to any of the foregoing bodies continue to be constables in their own forces retaining all of the privileges and status of the office. On completion of the secondment they return to their own police force (section 97).

Association of Chief Police Officers of England, Wales and Northern Ireland (ACPO)

(Note that there is a separate Scottish Organisation (ACPOS) that works closely with the Association.)

ACPO was formed in 1948 from previously existing bodies. It has no statutory recognition and is, in legal terms, an informal organisation.

The membership of ACPO comprises the chief officers of all English, Welsh and Northern Irish police forces, that is to say, all police officers who hold a rank above that of chief superintendent.

The Association was re-organised in 1968, and has a full-time secretariat funded by the Home Office. From about the mid-1970s it started to take a more prominent role in the formulation of police policies. The objectives of the ACPO are:

- to promote the welfare and efficiency of the police service and safeguard the interests of members of the Association;

- to provide opportunities for discussion and to give advice on matters affecting the police service;
- to provide social amenities for its members.

Nowadays the social role of ACPO has declined and the 'professional' side of the Association's activities has grown, most of this 'professional' work being performed through the Council of the Association.

The Council consists of the President and other officers of the Association, the commissioners of the Metropolitan and City of London police together with all of the chief constables of the police forces in England, Wales and Northern Ireland. All technical and professional matters are dealt with by the Council via one of its seven subsidiary specialist committees that cover:

- crime and CID matters;
- computer services;
- communications;
- traffic matters;
- training;
- technical services;
- general purposes.

Policing policies agreed within the ACPO will usually, in principle, be implemented in most of the police forces concerned.

Wide-scale co-operation between police forces was first brought to public attention when it was announced that arrangements had been made to set up and operate a National Reporting Centre (NRC). The centre, when activated, is placed under the command of the current President of ACPO and is designed to deal with incidents of national importance when mutual aid may be needed from many police forces. Subsequently the centre was renamed the Mutual Aid Co-ordinating Centre (MACC).

During the Miners' strike in 1984 the NRC oversaw and co-ordinated the arrangements for providing mutual aid between police forces throughout England and Wales. At the time, some political commentators claimed that the NRC was merely a 'cover arrangement' that permitted central government to exert direct control over all provincial police forces.

International organisations

International Criminal Police Organisation (INTERPOL)

This body was set up in 1923 with the object of helping to provide mutual assistance between the police authorities in different countries in the prevention and suppression of crime.

The General Secretariat in Paris co-ordinates the activities of police authorities of Member States in international matters and centralises records relating to the movement of international criminals.

The organisation particularly deals with international criminals:

- whose operations take place in more than one country;
- whose crimes are committed in one country but affect another country; or
- who commit crimes in one country but take refuge in another.

Each affiliated country has a domestic clearing house through which its individual police forces can communicate with the general secretariat or with the police of another country. The UK clearing house is controlled by the Metropolitan Police.

European Police Office (EUROPOL)

Article A, item 9 of the Maastricht Treaty 1992 instigated the organisation of a European Union wide system for exchanging information within a European Police Office (Europol). The information was concerned with police co-operation for the purposes of:

- preventing and combating terrorism;
- unlawful drug trafficking;
- dealing with other serious forms of international crime, including, if necessary, certain aspects of customs co-operation;

The above list of 'targets' will probably be extended as the office becomes more established.

Europol is located near to The Hague and currently has a staff of about 80 personnel. The office cannot work properly until at least a significant number of Member States ratify the treaty, UK was the first state to ratify in December 1996. The National Crime Intelligence Service, acting on behalf of all UK police forces, has established links with Europol.

Provision of advice and assistance to international organisations

A police authority may provide advice and assistance:

- to an international organisation or institution; or
- to any other person or body which is engaged outside the United Kingdom in the carrying on of activities similar to any carried on by the authority or the chief constable.

The power conferred on a police authority includes a power to make arrangements under which a member of the police force maintained by the authority is engaged for a period of temporary service with the international organisation or body. The police authority is not authorised to provide any financial assistance to the bodies concerned but may make charges for any advice or assistance provided (section 26).

These provisions do not affect any arrangements made under the Police (Overseas Service) Act 1945 and section 10 Overseas Development and Co-operation Act 1980.

4 Covert Policing

General

Historically, all modern states have had some sort of 'secret police' organisation. In totalitarian dictatorships the main purpose of these organisations has been to ensure the continued rule of the existing government by the elimination of political opposition. In most cases the secret police organisation has been given virtually unlimited authority that has far exceeded the democratic principle of the *rule of law*.

In democratic societies the activities of covert policing have been accepted with reluctance and there is continuous dispute about the accountability, authority and range of activities of those engaged in these activities.

Any activity that is secret always generates suspicion amongst those who are 'outsiders' for they will naturally suspect that some activities are against their best interests. Some individuals become quite paranoid about the covert activities that the press sometimes allege have occurred.

The problem is made worse by the 'insiders' who often adopt what can best be called a *conspiratorial ethos*. This results in excessive secrecy for its own sake and the non-disclosure of matters that might be embarrassing to individuals but which would certainly not put state security in any danger. This ill-founded secrecy leads to the conclusion that 'state security' is sometimes used as an excuse to suppress legitimate political criticism or prevent embarrassment of the government of the day.

Such suppression leads to a debate on the real extent of free expression in a country like the UK and the accountability of covert organs of state to the democratic process. Several writers have been strongly critical of what they refer to as 'political policing', notably Tony Bunyan, Peter Hain and Duncan Campbell. However, it is true to say that many people strongly disagree with their views.

The political pros and cons of the merits of covert policing is outside the scope of this handbook and if further details are needed they must be sought elsewhere, see source list for some books consulted by the author.

Changes in the activities of international criminals followed by changes in the law during the 1990s have resulted in covert methods being used in the fight against serious crime.

Covert police organisations in the UK

The Security Service

The UK Security Service (usually referred to in the press as MI5), was founded in 1909. It was firstly titled the Secret Service Bureau, later MO5, then MI5 and finally the Security Service. From 1909, for 80 years, it had no statutory basis, as its existence and activities were based upon the powers of the royal prerogative, see Chapter 1.

At its inception in 1909 the first tasks of the Security Service were to identify and deal with German agents conducting espionage in the UK. To provide greater power in this task the Official Secrets Act of 1911 was enacted to deal specifically with cases of espionage. Counter-espionage is still a major task of the Service. The general public knew little of the activities of this shadowy organisation and probably regarded them as 'the good guys' for the best part of 50 years.

During the 'cold war' from the 1950s to the 1970s a situation existed that called for the surveillance of people in sensitive positions who might have had communist sympathies. This was particularly important after a number of spy and defection scandals in the UK, USA and other Western countries.

There were many people of socialist views who would not have countenanced dealing with the old Soviet Union or its allies, but they were nonetheless targeted by the Security Service. Not unnaturally they resented this intrusion into their privacy and by the middle of the 1960s complaints about these surveillance activities were becoming more frequent.

The unease about 'political' policing became more widespread following serious scandals in Australia and New Zealand in the 1970s involving the Security Services and police Special Branches in those countries. These organisations were all based upon the British models in their organisation and modes of operation.

In each case they were found to have amassed large quantities of material that had little to do with the safety of the State, but showed obsessive collecting of tittle tattle as an end in itself (presumably 'just in case'). In both countries the actions were deemed to be unconstitutional, possibly even illegal and in consequence there were wholesale re-organisations of all aspects of security policing. The re-organisation included stricter controls on their activities and greater accountability to democratic representatives.

Canada, having similar organisations quickly took steps to control them by enacting the Canadian Security Intelligence Service Act 1984. This Act provides for a watchdog committee that includes representatives of all the major political parties in Parliament. Reporting to the committee is a government appointed Inspector General who is authorised to inspect all files of the Canadian Security Service. Anyone who obstructs the Inspector General in his tasks commits a criminal offence. These and other monitoring arrangements ensure that all intelligence activities in Canada are kept firmly under democratic control. This Canadian organisational pattern is the one usually advocated as a means of providing democratic control by people in other countries.

In UK the actions of the Security Service have always been limited by common law although many people have been convinced that its officers have been quite prepared to break the rules in their own secret interests.

Suspicion that security officers have regarded themselves as being above the ordinary laws of the land was given a factual basis in 1984 by an ex-Security Service Officer named Cathy Massiter. She revealed in a television programme that surveillance had been carried out on officials of the National Council for civil liberties that was deemed to be a subversive organisation.

Subsequently, the 'targeted' officials, Harriet Harmon and Patricia Hewitt claimed to the European Court of Human Rights that the actions of the Security Service had breached their right to privacy guaranteed by the European Convention of Human Rights. In 1990, the Human Rights Commission found that Article 8 of the Convention had been breached. The Commission said, in effect:

> An organisation with neither explicit legal powers or form could not lawfully invade an individual's privacy, nor keep secret files for essentially political purposes.

During the progress of the case, the UK government started to take steps to put the Security Service on to a statutory footing which included a system for the hearing of complaints made about the actions of its officers. As a result the Human Rights Commission felt that redress should be sought by Harmon and Hewitt in the UK by means of the authorised complaints Tribunal, see Chapter 14.

A major point raised by this case is the question how an organisation like the NCCL (now titled 'Liberty') could put the state in jeopardy. There is no doubt that 'Liberty' has, in the past, and will continue in the future to cause quite serious embarrassment to politicians and government officials given the nature of the cases that they pursue. However, treason is a very different thing to embarrassing politicians and officials.

In 1989 the Security Service Act was passed into law and the Service adopted a much higher public profile, the Director General made public speeches and a variety of publicity documents were subsequently produced.

A major policy change occurred in May 1992 when the Security Service took the lead position in gathering intelligence regarding Provisional IRA activities in mainland Britain, much to the disquiet of some police officers. However, subsequently the Security Service had its activities curtailed largely as a result of the diminishing of 'cold war' espionage activities by intelligence officers from Eastern European countries.

Following the announcement by the Provisional IRA of a 'cease-fire' on 31 August 1994, the Security Service assumed that its future activities would be even further reduced. They started to look for a new role as it was not predictable that the 'cease-fire' would only last for 17 months. The then Director General, Stella Rimmington, pressed for the involvement of the Security Service in intelligence gathering against organised criminal groups, especially those involved in drug trafficking and large-scale money laundering.

Several senior police officers expressed concern at the proposed extension of the Security Service's functions in this way because Security Service officers lack court experience. In the past, court proceedings have been undertaken by Police Special Branch officers thus allowing security officers to remain in the background.

Other people were also concerned with such a proposed extension into normal policing functions and objectors drew attention to the civil rights implications of Security Service involvement in criminal investigations. It was also pointed out that Security Service officers, unlike constables, do not possess personal prerogative power and accountability for their actions. Additionally, the Security Service as a whole is not accountable in anything like the same way that a police force is accountable to a democratic supervising authority, the press or the public in general.

There was much discussion in Parliament and eventually, in 1996, a further statute was enacted. This Act extended the duties of the Security Service to include intelligence gathering in cases of serious crime. It was emphasised in Parliament at the time that any action taken by the Security Service in respect of crime detection or prevention would be carried out *in support* of police forces and other law enforcement agencies (eg Customs and Excise).

Security Service Act 1989 as extended by the Security Service Act 1996 (SS Act)

The Security Service is under the authority of the Home Secretary (section 1 SS Act). The functions of the Security Service are (section 1 SS Act):

- the protection of national security and, in particular
  - protection against threats of espionage, terrorism and sabotage;
  - from the activities of agents of foreign powers; and
  - from actions intended to overthrow or undermine parliamentary democracy by political, industrial or violent means;
- to safeguard the economic well-being of the United Kingdom against threats posed by the actions or intentions of persons outside the British Islands;
- to act in support of the activities of police forces and other law enforcement agencies in the prevention and detection of serious crime. See below under warrants for definition of serious crime.

Operations of the Security Service are under control of a Director General appointed by the Home Secretary (section 2 SS Act).

The Director General is responsible for the efficiency of the Security Service and must ensure that:

- no information is obtained by the Security Service except what is necessary for the proper discharge of its functions;
- no information is to be disclosed except so far as necessary for discharging its functions or for preventing or detecting serious crime;
- no action is taken to further the interests of any political party;
- there are arrangements agreed with the Director General of the National Criminal Intelligence Service (section 12 PA 1997) for co-ordinating the

activities of the Security Service with the activities of police forces and other law enforcement agencies.

Information gathered by the Security Service can be used for security vetting purposes with the approval of the Home Secretary (section 2 SS Act).

The Director General must make an annual report on the work of the Security Service to the Prime Minister and the Home Secretary, additionally, he may at any time report to either of them on any matter relating to its work (section 2 SS Act).

The Act authorises the issue of warrants by the Home Secretary (section 3 SS Act) under the following terms:

- Entry on or interference with property is not unlawful if it is authorised by a warrant.
- Warrants may authorise the taking of any specified actions in respect of any property if it is needed to obtain information likely to be of substantial value and the information cannot reasonably be obtained by other means.
- Warrants may be issued during the investigation of crime if there are one or more offences, and either
  (a) it involves the use of violence, results in substantial financial gain or is conducted by a large number of persons in pursuit of a common purpose; or
  (b) the offence or one of the offences is an offence for which a person who has attained the age of 21 and has no previous convictions could reasonably be expected to be sentenced to imprisonment for a term of three years or more.
- Warrants are effective for six months, unless renewed by the Home Secretary.

During the progress of the Bill through Parliament it was said that warrants would not sanction any violence. Any Security Service Officer acting in pursuance of a warrant, if apprehended by a citizen would not resist, but would disclose the warrant on arrival at a police station. It would be unrealistic to suggest otherwise because, logically, if a covert surveillance operation becomes known to the target there is little point in carrying on with it in the same form.

Other intelligence services

The Intelligence Services Act 1994 makes statutory provision for the Secret Intelligence Service (SIS) often referred to in the press as MI6 and Government Communications Headquarters (GCHQ) in similar terms to those provided in the Security Service Act.

The main interest in the 1994 Act from a policing point of view is that it authorises the issue of warrants to monitor wireless telegraphy transmissions or tapping a wide range of telephones by GCHQ.

The Security Service, Secret Intelligence Service or GCHQ can all apply to the Home Secretary for warrants to intercept various communication links. Presumably the Security Service could use such a warrant when undertaking criminal investigations against organised crime syndicates.

The Police Special Branch

The Special Branch was formed in the Metropolitan Police in 1883 to track down the Fenian dynamiters of the Irish Republican Brotherhood. Initially this special squad of officers was referred to internally as the 'political branch', but this was deemed to be an unacceptable name, hence the eventual title of Special Branch.

Although the Special Branch of the Metropolitan Police still has national security responsibilities, every force has its own Special Branch operating in its own police area.

There has always been an air of mystique and secrecy about the Branch in the eyes of the public – which those officers serving in it probably encourage. For the same reasons that caused public disquiet about the secret activities of the Security Service, the Special Branch was also subjected to public criticism for its activities.

By about 1980, after the Australian and New Zealand upsets, some chief constables were becoming concerned about the 'bad press' that the Special Branches in UK police forces were attracting and started to take steps to allay public anxiety.

In 1982, John Alderson, then Chief Constable of Devon and Cornwall, took the lead and publicly ordered that the local Special Branch files should be weeded out. Several hundred files had been collected during the preceding 20 years, and it was suggested that of all these files only about 20 had real relevance. Alderson said at the time:

> I've found, by making checks on the activities of my officers, that there is this innate tendency to want to record almost anything, however remotely connected it may be with activity which might in the loosest sense be regarded as subversive. The word 'subversive' needs to be defined ... Some people would regard subversion as anything which is designed to change society.

Many other chief constables followed suit, although they did not necessarily court the same publicity as Alderson. Some Special Branch officers tried to avoid supervision by their chief constables, but quickly learned that the chief constable really does direct and control the force as stated in the Police Act.

There have been a number of examples of improper and/or incorrect information kept on file by Special Branch. One such case occurred in the late 1970s when a Mrs Jan Martin learned that she was categorised as a security risk because of possible links with the Baader-Meinhof terrorist group and for 18 months was unable to obtain work. Fortunately for Mrs Martin her father was a retired Chief Superintendent of Police and he was able to pursue the matter.

In March 1981 the Metropolitan Police issued a statement saying:

> In October 1978 it came to our notice as a result of representations from Mrs Martin's father that an inquiry about a motor car seen in Holland in 1977, and subsequently found to be owned by Mrs Martin, had not been completed as quickly and efficiently as it should have been. This was rectified and regret was expressed by a senior officer to Mrs Martin, who was completely innocent of any offence, for any embarrassment caused.

The police statement went on to say:

> Some information about the inquiry inadvertently had been communicated to a commercial company and the Special Branch Officer responsible was given strict advice and administrative action was taken to guard against any repetition of such an incident.

> **Officers were reminded that improper disclosure of information could be an offence under the Official Secrets Act, and would most certainly amount to a discipline offence.**

[Emphasis added.]

In 1983 West Midlands Special Branch placed a woman under investigation for writing a letter to a newspaper in which she said 'the only way to stop cruise missile bases being established in Britain is by peaceful demonstration'. The problem in this case was that the local police force denied any knowledge of the investigation. About a year later it was publicly admitted that a detective constable of the Special Branch had been involved in the matter and an apology was given.

Public disquiet about the activities of the Security Service naturally enough embraced the activities of the Special Branch and in 1985 the Commons home affairs select committee investigated and reported upon Special Branch activities. The committee consisted of seven Conservative and four Labour MPs and the eventual report showed the committee divided on party lines. The four Labour MPs and their colleagues in the House claimed that the report was a 'whitewash' and they presented a minority report.

The report said that there was little doubt that the Special Branches have been in danger of acquiring a sinister reputation of a force which persecutes harmless citizens for political reasons, acts in nefarious ways to assist the security services and is accountable to no one. The report said at one point:

> We believe that chief constables do, through appropriate senior officers, exercise the same degree of control over their Special Branches as they do over all police officers.

The minority report referred to the various complaints made about Special Branch officers and suggested that an independent commission of inquiry should be set up to investigate the Special Branch.

During the early stages of the committee's inquiry the Home Secretary published the guidelines for Special Branch work and the committee commented that it was not clear why they had been kept secret for so long.

The guidelines, re-issued in July 1994 under the title 'Guidelines on Special Branch Work in Great Britain' set the parameters for Special Branch activities.

The guidelines define the fundamental principles as:

- each Special Branch remains an integral part of the local force, accountable to individual chief officers and available for them to deploy on any duties flowing from their responsibility for the preservation of the Queen's peace, including the prevention and detection of crime;

- Special Branches make a crucial contribution to the protection of national security including, in particular, counter-terrorist work, through their close co-operation with the Security Service;
- Special Branch officers are bound by the same disciplinary code as other police officers and have no additional legal powers by virtue of their employment within Special Branch.

The functions of the Special Branch

Special Branches exist primarily to acquire intelligence, to assess its potential operational value, and to contribute more generally to its interpretation. They do so both to meet local policing needs and also to assist the Security Service in carrying out its statutory duty under the Security Service Act 1989 – namely the protection of national security and, in particular, protection against threats from espionage, terrorism, and sabotage, from the activities of agents of foreign powers and from actions intended to overthrow or undermine parliamentary democracy by political, industrial or violent means. The Security Service provides advice to chief officers about its particular requirements for assistance in their force area.

Surveillance and a citizen's right to privacy

Statutory protection of communication

Most citizens are apprehensive of an Orwellian 'Big Brother' exerting secret control over them. The wish for privacy and the dislike of those who 'spy' has long been part of the British mentality.

Under the Justices of the Peace Act 1361 'listening at the eaves of a house' was deemed to be a breach of the peace – as recently as 1948 the authority of this old statute was upheld (*R v London Quarter Sessions ex parte Metropolitan Police Commissioner* (1948)). Several later statutes protect communication from unauthorised interference or examination, in brief they are:

Wireless Telegraphy Act 1949
Makes offences for an unauthorised person to use wireless telegraphy apparatus with intent to obtain information as to the content, sender or addressee of any message that he is not authorised to receive.

Post Office Act 1953
Makes a series of offences for taking, retaining or diverting postal packets and for post office officials to steal, destroy, open or delay postal packets.

Interception of Communications Act 1985
Makes offences of intentionally intercepting a communication in the course of transmission by postal or public telecommunication services.

Computer Misuse Act 1990
Makes offences of gaining unauthorised access to or tampering with programs or data held on a computer.

Authorised surveillance

The law can provide authority for covert policing which will include the surveillance of communications. An early example is:

Official Secrets Act 1920

Requires persons carrying on the business of receiving postal packets to be registered with the chief officer of police and keep a book showing:

- the name and address of every person for whom postal packets are received;
- any instructions for forwarding or delivering postal packets;
- the place from which the postal packet came, date of postmark, date of receipt and name and address of sender if shown on the packet together with details of registration when applicable;
- date of delivery or forwarding of packet and to whom delivered or forwarded;
- the person receiving or forwarding the packet to sign a receipt.

The book, instructions for dealing with packets and packets held to be made available for inspection by a constable at all reasonable times.

At the time, 1920, most communication was carried on by post. It was not until many years later that other forms of communication became commonplace. The Act remains in force but does not appear to cause any concern nowadays.

Since the end of the Second World War there has been an increasing use of modern technology and criminals have not been slow in taking advantage of the facilities offered. To allow lawful monitoring of these communications the Security Service and police have been granted warrants, usually by the Home Secretary. Initially warrants used the authority of the *royal prerogative*, but as the law developed, statutory authorities became available. The three Acts:

Wireless Telegraphy Act 1949

Interception of Communications Act 1985

Computer Misuse Act 1990

all permit the issue of warrants to authorise the interception of communications by specific official bodies such as the police, customs and excise, security and intelligence services.

Surveillance devices such as receiver/transmitter 'bugs'; directional microphones; optical fibre devices; long focus camera lenses and the other technological paraphernalia of modern surveillance techniques are not specifically banned by law. Indeed many of these devices are used by journalists and private inquiry agents. Although there is no specific law of privacy, improper use of information gained by surveillance techniques could be in breach of particular laws such as the Data Protection Act 1984 as amended.

The Security Service Act 1989 and the Intelligence Services Act 1994 authorise the Home Secretary to issue warrants to all of the intelligence services. The warrants can permit entry onto and interference with property for the purpose of using surveillance equipment when they are carrying out their functions.

Surveillance activities by police, including Special Branches are authorised by section 92 Police Act 1997. It is best illustrated by diagram as shown below:

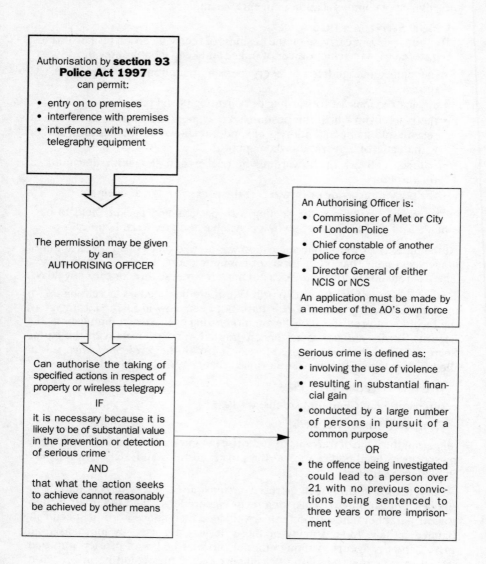

Authorisation by **section 93 Police Act 1997** can permit:

- entry on to premises
- interference with premises
- interference with wireless telegraphy equipment

The permission may be given by an AUTHORISING OFFICER

An Authorising Officer is:

- Commissioner of Met or City of London Police
- Chief constable of another police force
- Director General of either NCIS or NCS

An application must be made by a member of the AO's own force

Can authorise the taking of specified actions in respect of property or wireless telegraphy

IF

it is necessary because it is likely to be of substantial value in the prevention or detection of serious crime

AND

that what the action seeks to achieve cannot reasonably be achieved by other means

Serious crime is defined as:

- involving the use of violence
- resulting in substantial financial gain
- conducted by a large number of persons in pursuit of a common purpose

OR

- the offence being investigated could lead to a person over 21 with no previous convictions being sentenced to three years or more imprisonment

In some cases, the Authorising Officer must get the approval of Commissioners appointed for the purpose of overseeing these activities, these cases are:

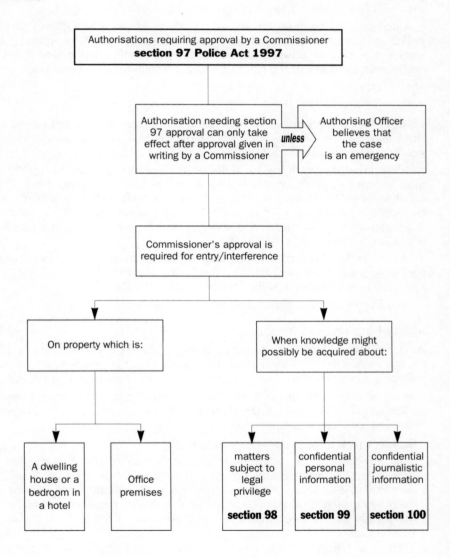

If a Commissioner refuses to approve an authorisation made under section 97 Police Act 1997 he must make a report to the Authorising Officer concerned giving his reasons for the refusal. The Authorising Officer may then appeal to the Chief Commissioner for the decision to be reversed, see page 121.

Authorisations by chief constables or other Authorising Officers giving police officers permission to enter or interfere with property, etc must be in writing unless the case is urgent. In such cases the authorisation can be given orally (section 95 PA 1997). Authorisations are valid for a maximum of:

- oral authorisation   72 hours;
- written authorisation   3 months.

However, an authorisation can be renewed in writing for a further period of three months. As soon as the actions originally approved are no longer necessary the authorisation must be cancelled.

When an authorisation is given, renewed or cancelled the Authorising Officer must inform a Commissioner in writing as soon as reasonably practicable. This notification will state whether section 97 is applicable to the particular case (section 96 PA 1997). In the absence of an Authorising Officer another designated officer, as specified in the Act, will be empowered to authorise police actions (section 94 PA 1997).

The Home Secretary must issue a *code of practice* to be followed by persons performing functions authorised by the Police Act 1997. The code must be approved by both Houses of Parliament (section 101 PA 1997).

See Chapter 14 for further details on Commissioners.

Right of privacy

As stated above, there is no general statutory right to personal privacy in this country so reliance for a legal authority to such a right is usually based on the European Convention for the Protection of Human Rights, see Appendix A.

Using the Convention as a legal basis, there have been several cases challenging the right of the state to infringe the privacy of individual citizens. Following are some significant decisions.

Malone v Metropolitan Commissioner (1979)

This was the first case of importance in this area of law. Malone was prosecuted for handling stolen goods and during the trial the prosecution admitted that his telephone had been tapped on the authority of a Home Secretary's warrant. Malone claimed that the tapping was unlawful and he had a right to privacy in accordance with Article 8 of the Human Rights Convention.

The court held that the phone tapping was not illegal and that the Convention did not give any enforceable rights under English law. Malone's case was rejected.

Malone then took his case to the European Commission for Human Rights with the following result:

Malone v UK (1985)

The Court of Human Rights held that in UK law:

- the lack of definition of the circumstances under which tapping could be carried out; and
- the absence of any means for remedying any abuse of power

meant that the phone tapping in this case was not carried out in accordance with the Human Rights Convention.

As a direct result of this judgment the Interception of Communications Act 1985 was enacted so that surveillance warrants would henceforth be on a statutory footing.

Several challenges were later made questioning the legality of various aspects of 'tapping'. Following are the most important decisions.

R v Effick (1992)
R v Mitchell (1992)

These cases went to the Court of Appeal. In them the prosecution gave detailed evidence of telephone calls between a third party using a cordless telephone and Effick and Mitchell. The calls were tape-recorded and suggested that both were involved in the supply of drugs. No warrant for interception had been obtained. The court held that the presiding judge had discretion to allow such evidence if he considered it right so to do. In this case he exercised his discretion reasonably and the convictions stood.

R v Bailey and Smith (1993)

In this case, Bailey and Smith had been charged with conspiracy to commit robberies but they remained silent during interview. They were remanded in custody to await an identification parade and the police officers obtained permission to install listening equipment in the remand cell. In the cell Bailey and Smith engaged in conversations that included a number of admissions. The tape-recording of these admissions was allowed in evidence at their subsequent trial. The Appeal Court upheld the convictions and said that, as the legislation and codes presently (1993) stood, there was neither unlawfulness in the obtaining, nor unfairness in the admitting, of the taped conversations.

R v Ahmed (1995)

Following the arrest of Ahmed and another for drugs offences they were allowed to make telephone calls on a pay phone in the police station. Police became suspicious at the number of calls so a monitoring device was installed on the internal switchboard. The tape-recorded conversations were later used in the prosecution's case for conspiracy to supply controlled drugs. It was claimed on appeal that the evidence was inadmissible because no warrant under the Interception of Communications Act 1985 had been obtained, therefore the monitoring was unlawful. The Court of Appeal held that the 1985 Act only applies to calls made on a public telephone system. In this case the calls were still on a private system up to the point where they left the police station switchboard for onward transmission. The appeals were rejected.

A subsequent European Court of Human Rights judgment is in conflict with the *Ahmed* case in the following particulars:

Halford v United Kingdom (1997)

Former assistant chief constable Alison Halford was pursuing a case of discrimination against her chief constable. Whilst this was proceeding her office telephone at police headquarters was monitored and she claimed that this infringed her privacy contrary to Article 8 of the Convention. The Court of Human Rights accepted that neither the Interception of Communications Act nor any other law existed to regulate internal communication systems. However, as no legal authority existed, the interference of Halford's telephone constituted a breach of her privacy as defined in Article 8. Further, as the interference was not specifically authorised by law, Halford had no avenue of redress under domestic English law in order to make her complaint. Under these circumstances her rights under Article 13 had also been violated.

See Appendix A for Convention details.

There appears to be a conflict between *Ahmed* and *Halford* in the context of acceptability of evidence and this will probably have to be resolved by a change in legislation, perhaps by extending the provisions of the Interception of Communications Act to private communication systems.

It was reported that West Yorkshire police carried out surveillance on a suspected drug trafficker named Govell. A spy-hole for a device was drilled in the wall of his house and evidence acquired through this device was used in his prosecution. Govell was sentenced to 10 years' imprisonment and subsequently challenged (unsuccessfully) this invasion of privacy by way of judicial review.

R v Khan (Sultan) (1996)

In this case Khan and his cousin Nawab were stopped on leaving a flight at Manchester Airport. Nawab had in his possession £100,000 worth of heroin and was detained, charged and later prosecuted. Khan had nothing incriminating in his possession nor did he make any incriminating statement, he was therefore released after interview. Later Khan visited the home of a man called Bashforth in Sheffield where South Yorkshire police had installed an electronic listening device on the external wall of Bashforth's house. This permitted conversations in the living room to be monitored and tape-recorded and, largely on the basis of these recordings, Khan was charged and convicted of a drugs offence for which he was sentenced to three years' imprisonment.

The House of Lords said that in English law, in general, there is nothing unlawful about breach of privacy. Khan's case rested wholly upon the lack of statutory authorisation for the police action and the court held that evidence obtained in this way is admissible at the discretion of the presiding judge. Khan's appeal was dismissed and it was observed by Lord Nolan that: 'It would be a strange reflection on our law if a man who had admitted his participation in the illegal importation of a large quantity of heroin should have his conviction set aside on the ground that his privacy had been invaded.'

The *Khan* case is a House of Lords' decision that can only be altered by an Act of Parliament and, unless Parliament decides to alter the law, any evidence similarly obtained is admissible at the discretion of the presiding judge. It was later reported that both Govell and Khan have instituted proceedings in the European Court of Human Rights for alleged breaches of Article 8. In two later cases, *R v Rasool* (1997) and *R v Choudhary* (1997), the Court of Appeal cited the *Effick* (1992) case as giving the general construction of the law.

Legal liability of surveillance officers

A point of significance in respect of surveillance duties was made as an aside during the case involving the ex Security Officer, Peter Wright and his book *Spycatcher*. During the House of Lords appeal Lord Justice Templeman said:

> No member of the Secret Service is immune from criminal prosecution or civil suit in respect of his actions. Instructions from superior officers are no defence.

This is clear and unequivocal, officers engaged on surveillance duties must conform to all aspects of both criminal and civil law, and every action must have a clear legal authorisation, either by a warrant or otherwise.

Part II

The institutional authorities that control policing activity

The office of chief constable

The 'man in charge' (today it is sometimes the 'woman in charge') of the formative police forces had a variety of titles in the 19th century such as *captain of the watch, superintending constable, head constable* and from about the 1880s onwards the title of *chief constable* which became universal in 1919.

Before the wholesale amalgamations of small police forces in the 1960s there was a vast difference in the power exercised by chief constables in charge of the smallest forces compared with those who controlled the big city and county forces. Nowadays all chief constables control large organisations with budgets of many millions of pounds and as such the position carries with it a lot of power together with an equal level of responsibility towards the public he serves.

The basic outline of a chief constable's legal position is contained in the Police Act, but due to the complexities of his office it is also necessary to review a number of judicial decisions in order to see the whole picture.

All provincial police forces are under the direction and control of an appointed chief constable, who, in carrying out the functions of his office, must pay regard to the local policing plan that has been issued by the police authority for his area (section 10).

The chief constable is responsible for the appointment, promotion and discipline of members of his force who are below the rank of assistant chief constable (sections 13 and 67 to 76). He is answerable, in discipline terms, to his police authority (section 68), see Chapter 13.

Appointment of the chief constable

The chief constable is appointed by the police authority responsible for maintaining the force, but subject to the approval of the Home Secretary and to regulations made under the Police Act (section 11).

A short list of candidates drawn up before an appointment must be approved by the Home Secretary. There have been cases when the Home Secretary and a police authority have failed to agree regarding potential appointees. Following are some recent examples:

In 1990, the Derbyshire police committee wished to appoint Deputy Chief Constable John Weselby to the post of chief constable but the Home Secretary would not agree to the appointment. The police authority stated their intention of seeking a judicial review of the Home Secretary's veto, however, the impasse was resolved when Mr Weselby eventually withdrew his candidature for the post.

In 1994, the North Wales police authority sought to have Deputy Chief Constable John Tecwyn Owen promoted to Chief Constable because he was the only Welsh speaking candidate on the short list. However, the Home Secretary again vetoed the proposal and another officer was duly appointed.

Removal of the chief constable from office

The police authority, acting with the approval of the Home Secretary, may call upon the chief constable to retire in the interests of efficiency or effectiveness (section 11). The Home Secretary is authorised to direct a police authority to make use of this power (section 42).

Following are cases relating to the use of these powers:

The last occasion that a police authority removed a chief constable was the dismissal of Stanley Parr in 1977. The Lancashire Police Authority authorised an inquiry into Parr's conduct by another chief constable. In the ensuing disciplinary tribunal he was found guilty on 26 counts of misconduct and was dismissed from the Force.

In 1985 the Home Secretary required the Derbyshire Police Authority to retire Chief Constable Alfred Parrish in the interest of efficiency. Mr Parrish had been suspended following alleged irregularities in the spending of police funds.

Once appointed, it is almost impossible to remove a chief constable other than for corruption or serious misconduct and, providing he retains the support of the Home Secretary, the police authority will not be able to remove him.

This was shown, and reported widely in the local press when the Merseyside Police Authority called upon Chief Constable Oxford to resign in 1985. His reply, quoted in the press, was 'I have every Christian virtue except resignation'. As Mr Oxford retained the support of the Home Secretary his remark summed up the security of his position.

If, because of disagreements on policing policy, a police authority removed a chief constable with the Home Secretary's support, the action would be open to challenge in the courts. The challenge would lie in the grounds that the dismissal was based on things other than his efficiency or effectiveness. Additionally, if the force had been awarded its annual certificate of efficiency (see page 96), it is difficult to see how a claim that he lacked efficiency or effectiveness in his operational control could be sustained.

Assistant chief constables

The police authority must appoint, after consultation with the chief constable, and subject to the approval of the Home Secretary, at least one person as an assistant chief constable (section 12). The appointment, removal and discipline of assistant chief constables follow the same procedures as for the chief constable (sections 12 and 68).

The chief constable, after consulting the police authority, shall designate one of the assistant chief constables to exercise the powers and duties of the chief constable during his absence or during any vacancy in the office (section 12). No more than one person can be designated to act as deputy chief constable.

The appointed person cannot act as chief constable for a longer continuous period than three months, unless the Home Secretary so consents (section 12).

The position of deputy chief constable is an appointment, not a specific rank which is a reversion to the pre-1984 arrangements.

Reports by the chief constable

To the police authority

Before each financial year the chief constable must prepare and submit a draft local policing plan for the consideration of the police authority (section 8). Additionally, the police authority, in consultation with the chief constable must establish local policing objectives for the forthcoming year (section 7). For further details see page 65.

As soon as possible after the end of each financial year, the chief constable must prepare a general report for the police authority. The report will provide information regarding the policing of the area during that year (section 22). Copies of this report must also be submitted to the Home Secretary (section 44) and be published appropriately (section 22).

The chief constable shall, whenever required by the police authority, submit a report, in the form specified, on matters connected with the policing of the force area (section 22).

How far the police authority could go in demanding reports (under the terms of the Police Act 1919) was raised in Nottingham in a 1957 incident:

The Chief Constable, Captain Athelstan Popkess, believed that certain members of the City Council were guilty of corruption. After taking advice from the Director of Public Prosecutions, Captain Popkess arranged for an investigation to be undertaken by detectives from the Metropolitan Police but following receipt of the report the Director decided to take no further action.

Nottingham Watch Committee instructed Captain Popkess to report to them on the inquiries but he refused to do so on the grounds that dealing with criminal matters was his responsibility and not within the jurisdiction of the Watch Committee.

The Watch Committee then suspended the Chief Constable from duty using as their authority the Municipal Corporations Act 1835. The Home Secretary, using the precedents of *Fisher v Oldham Corporation* (1930) and *AG New South Wales v Perpetual Trustee Co* (1955), together with the Crown's prerogative duty to maintain law and order stated that he could not accept the suspension of the Chief Constable. The Watch Committee reinstated the Chief Constable and did not pursue the matter through the courts.

[See pages 15 and 16 for details of quoted cases.]

Under the existing Police Act the matter is clarified. It is laid down that if it appears to the chief constable that a report in compliance with a requirement

55

would contain information which in the public interest ought not to be disclosed, or is not needed for the discharge of the functions of the police authority, he may request the authority to refer the requirement to the Home Secretary. In any such case the requirement shall be of no effect unless it is confirmed by the Home Secretary (section 22).

The practical effect of this requirement is to make it very difficult for a police authority to judge the effectiveness or efficiency of their chief constable. This is because they are entirely dependent upon the willingness of the chief constable to give information about details of operational matters or upon the Home Secretary to confirm the requirement.

Other members of the police force would be precluded from giving any information that had already been refused by the chief constable as they would be in jeopardy of prosecution for an offence under the Official Secrets Acts together with action under the discipline regulations.

To the Home Secretary

If required so to do, the chief constable will make a report to the Home Secretary on any specified matter concerned with the policing of his area and he will make arrangements to publish the report (section 44).

The chief constable must send a copy of his annual report prepared for the police authority to the Home Secretary (section 44).

The chief constable must transmit crime statistics in the force area to the Home Secretary, they will contain details of:

- offences;
- offenders;
- criminal proceedings; and
- the state of crime in the area.

The Home Secretary will make a consolidated abstract of all of the information received from police forces and will lay it before parliament (section 45).

Chief constables have been required to submit crime statistics to the Home Secretary since 1856. Originally these data together with demographic information were the main considerations in deciding the establishment of police forces and thereby the amount of the Exchequer grant paid to them. The grant was also first authorised in 1856.

The validity of the submitted crime statistics began to be seriously questioned in the late 1970s when it was claimed, in essence, that the number of crimes recorded by the police was lower than those actually committed. Similarly it was claimed that the clear up rate of detected crimes was also overstated.

In 1982 the first British Crime Survey was undertaken by the Home Office and this revealed a considerable variation in some categories of crime between the figure recorded by the police and the figure assessed by the survey. Several subsequent surveys by other agencies came to similar conclusions although there were some differences in the actual figures.

These surveys heightened the debate and caused questions to be asked about the assessment of the efficiency of police forces based upon data that they themselves had produced. The climax came in the middle of 1986 with press headlines such as 'Crime figures scandal' caused by the following events:

In January 1986 a detective constable of Kent Constabulary went to the Metropolitan Police to complain that Kent detectives were routinely falsifying crime reports to improve the apparent efficiency of their own sections. This was the information revealed to the press later in the year.

The Police Complaints Authority forthwith initiated a full investigation into the activities of these detectives – the investigation was long drawn out because numerous files were mislaid or missing when required by the investigating officers. Eventually, in September 1989, three years and eight months after the initial report, one detective was dismissed from the force and 34 others were subject to other disciplinary action.

This incident confirmed the suspicions of many people about the veracity of crime statistics produced by the police and it led to a change in funding procedures. Now the allocation of the Exchequer grant is based on a complex formula that includes a range of data acquired from sources additional to police produced statistics.

The status of chief constable

The status of the chief constable is not made clear in statute law. However, in the same way that the status of a constable has been defined, a number of leading cases have considered the issues concerning this matter.

R v Metropolitan Police Commissioner ex parte Blackburn (1968)

The authority of the Commissioner of the Metropolitan Police and police in general was outlined by Denning MR, as follows:

… His constitutional status has never been defined either by statute or by the courts … I have no hesitation, however, in holding that, like every constable in the land, he should be, and is, independent of the executive. He is not subject to the orders of the Secretary of State, save that under the Police Act, 1964 the Secretary of State can call on him to give a report, or to retire in the interests of efficiency.

I hold it to be the duty of the Commissioner of Police, as it is of every Chief Constable, to enforce the law of the land. He must take steps so to post his men that crimes may be detected; and that honest citizens may go about their affairs in peace. He must decide whether or not suspected persons are to be prosecuted; and, if need be, bring the prosecution or see that it is brought; but in all these things he is not the servant of anyone, save the law itself.

No Minister of the Crown can tell him that he must, or must not, keep observation on this place; or that he must, or must not, prosecute this man or that one. Nor can any police authority tell him so. He is answerable to the law and to the law alone …

Although the chief officers of police are answerable to the law, there are many fields in which they have a discretion with which the law will not interfere. For instance, it is for the Commissioner of Police, or the chief constable, as the case may be, to decide in any particular case whether enquiries should be pursued, or whether an arrest should be made, or a prosecution brought. It must be for him to decide on the disposition of his force and the concentration of his resources on any particular crime or area. No court can or should give him direction on such a matter.

He can also make policy decisions and give effect to them, as for instance, was often done when prosecutions were not brought for attempted suicide; but there are some policy decisions with which, I think, the courts in a case can, if necessary interfere. Suppose a chief constable were to issue a directive to his men that no person should be prosecuted for stealing any goods less than £100 in value. I should have thought that the court would countermand it. He would be failing in his duty to enforce the law ...

[The duty of prosecution now rests with the Crown Prosecution Service.]

R v Metropolitan Police Commissioner ex parte Blackburn and another (1973)

This was an application for *mandamus* to direct the Commissioner to enforce the Obscene Publications Act 1959. The application was dismissed and the court stated that it would interfere only in the extreme case where a Commissioner was not carrying out his duty of enforcing the law; it would not interfere with the discretion which the Commissioner had in carrying out that duty.

R v Oxford ex parte Levey (1986)

The same standard of policing could not be universally applied. The chief constable had to look at the circumstances and adapt the policy accordingly. Where a chief constable, in the exercise of his discretion had adopted a policing method that was not shown to be ineffective or in breach of his duty to keep the peace and enforce the law, the court would not review the chief constable's choice of policing method.

R v Secretary of State for the Home Department ex parte Northumbria Police Authority (1987)

A court would not intervene to control the use that a chief constable made of the resources available to him. (This case related to plastic baton rounds and CS gas equipment.)

[For further details of this case see page 68.]

Public authorities, including chief constables, must uphold the 'rule of law' when performing their functions as was stated in the following case.

R v Coventry Airport Ltd ex parte Phoenix Aviation and other applications (1995)

This case followed the activities of animal rights protesters who sought to stop the exports of live animals. The local authority owners of Coventry Airport decided to suspend the flights carrying livestock exports because of the public disorder. The livestock exporters sought judicial review of the decision.

The High Court held that the local authority had no discretion under the founding legislation to impose such a ban, further, even if such a discretion existed, public disorder would not have provided appropriate grounds for imposing such a ban. To permit the local authority to rely upon the threat of unlawful public disorder by animal rights protesters as the basis for banning the export of animals for slaughter would be to undermine the rule of law.

The impact of European law on the operational discretion of a chief constable was raised following extensive disorder caused by demonstrators trying to prevent livestock being exporting through Shoreham in Sussex. The chief constable decided to provide no policing to protect the transport of livestock to the port of Shoreham for shipment to France save on two consecutive days a week or four consecutive days a fortnight excluding in any case Fridays, weekends or bank holidays. The underlying reason for the restriction was the increasing cost of deploying scarce police resources to deal with one continuing incident and he refused to alter this decision when requested so to do by the exporters.

ITF, the transport company, sought judicial review in the High Court where it was held that the chief constable's actions had the effect of restricting exports and therefore breached the European Union Treaty. It was also said that providing the resources were available to deal with such disturbances and the cost of doing so was not disproportionate the chief constable could not rely on the 'public policy' defence of the Treaty. The chief constable's decision was quashed but he appealed to the Court of Appeal.

R v Chief Constable of Sussex ex parte International Traders' Ferry Ltd (1997)

It was held that the chief constable was not only entitled, but in fact obliged, to use his available resources to police as well as he could the area for which he was responsible. If that was his aim then proper policing was obviously a public policy aim as countenanced by the Treaty. Kennedy LJ said:

> The chief constable had to balance at least three competing rights and interests, namely:
>
> 1 ITF's right to protection for its lawful economic activity;
>
> 2 the right of the residents of Sussex to protection from crime and disorder; and
>
> 3 the right of animal rights protesters to protest peacefully, but not illegally.

With unlimited resources, manpower and finance, there would be no competition between the rights but the court did not require evidence in order to be satisfied that the resources were not infinite. If a balance had to be struck it almost inevitably followed that no one right or interest could be regarded as absolute.

The chief constable clearly did strike a balance, and it was European law as well as domestic law that no court would interfere with his decision unless it could be shown that he was plainly wrong. The chief constable's order was reinstated.

[Emphasis added.]

The question of the availability of resources was also raised in a House of Lords' decision:

R v Gloucestershire County Council and another ex parte Barry (1997)

Here it was held that the availability of resources, including the cost, is a proper consideration when deciding on the provision of services.

Subsequent cases have accepted the same principle.

Since 1994 the Home Secretary has been empowered by statute to define policing objectives and performance targets (sections 37 and 38), but he cannot direct the chief constable on the operational methods used to implement these matters.

The regulation of his force

The chief constable's internal regulation of his force can be questioned in the courts as was illustrated in a case brought by the Police Federation regarding the number of police officers appointed to fulfil particular duties prescribed by law.

Vince and another v Chief Constable of Dorset (1993)

A chief constable is not under a statutory duty under section 36 of the Police And Criminal Evidence Act 1984 to appoint a sufficient number of custody officers to ensure that at each designated police station there will ordinarily be available a custody officer to perform the functions of custody officers. A chief constable's duty under section 36 is to appoint one custody officer for each designated police station with a discretion, which must be exercised reasonably, to appoint more than one custody officer if he considers it right to do so.

See the use of discretion under the heading *ultra vires* doctrine on page 104 *et seq*.

Insofar as the Health and Safety at Work Act 1974 and regulations made thereunder are concerned, the chief constable is considered to be the employer of all constables and police cadets (Police (Health and Safety) Act 1997).

Additional points

As the duties, responsibilities and powers of the chief constable are imprecisely defined this has been an area of great controversy. A phrase that has come into wide use by the police service, central government and some police authorities is that **chief constables exercise operational control**. This phrase appears nowhere in the legislation nor in any legal source. As a result it is seen by some critics as the means of restricting democratic control over police forces.

It is also questionable how far 'direction and control' extend to financial matters. Certainly it does not include the power to provide funds that is clearly a duty of the police authority, but it must include the manner of some expenditure, which is also a responsibility of the police authority. See the Northumbria case later regarding this point (page 68). In the current climate of financial stringency in public spending it could be suggested that one measurement of the efficiency and effectiveness of a chief constable could be the manner in which he deploys the financial resources allocated to his force.

National bodies

The Directors General of the National Criminal Intelligence Service and the National Crime Squad are both appointed to the police rank of chief constable. It is probable, that if questions are raised regarding the command and control of their respective organisations, they will be regarded as having a similar relationship as that which exists between a provincial chief constable and his force.

6　The Police Authority

The establishment of police authorities

During the first half of the 19th century local police forces in towns and cities were controlled by *watch committees*, the title being directly connected to the Statute of Winchester 1285. County police forces were controlled initially by the county justices and later by a *standing joint committee* that consisted of both justices and county councillors.

Since the 1960s the pattern of police forces has changed enormously and consequently the format of what are now titled *police authorities* has also changed. Nonetheless, the long-established principle of exercising control over the police at a local level has continued.

The legal basis of a police authority is contained in the Police Act which directs that a police authority will be established as a statutory corporate body in each police area (section 3).

Police authorities are independent of other local government bodies but they are subject to the same statutory controls in their general procedures and the standards that are expected from their members (section 21 and Local Government Acts).

Membership of police authorities

Each police authority consists of 17 members (section 4) constituted as follows:
- nine elected councillors from the county(ies) policed by the force;
- five independent members (approved by the Home Secretary); and
- three magistrates from the county(ies) policed by the force.

The Home Secretary can alter the number of members in the police authority of a particular force area if it is considered appropriate so to do (sections 4 and 5).

The composition of the authority, appointment of its members and details on the form of its proceedings are contained in Schedules 2 and 3.

Statutory appointments

The police authority, subject to the approval of the Home Secretary, is responsible for the appointment, removal and discipline of their chief constable and at least one assistant chief constable (sections 11, 12, 42 and 68).

The police authority must appoint a person to be the clerk to the authority (section 16). This person, or any other appointment required by law, may or may not be an employee of the authority (section 17). A person appointed as the clerk or to any other statutory civilian appointment, will not be under the direction and control of the chief constable (section 15).

Discipline authority

The police authority is the lawful discipline authority for its chief constable and assistant chief constable(s). Discipline processes must be carried out in conformity with Part IV Police Act 1996 and any regulations made thereunder.

The police authority must keep themselves informed as to the working of the discipline procedures in respect of their police force (section 77).

Police fund

The police authority must keep a fund to be known as the police fund (section 14). All receipts of the police authority must be paid into this fund, all expenditure must be paid out of it and full accounts must be kept concerning all these transactions, see further details in Chapter 9.

The functions of police authorities

It is the duty of the police authority to secure the maintenance of an efficient and effective police force for the area (section 6). In providing a police force the authority must pay regard to all the following:

- any policing objectives determined by the Home Secretary;
- local policing objectives;
- local performance targets;
- the local policing plan issued by the authority;
- any codes of practice issued by the Home Secretary; and
- any direction authorised by the Police Act and issued by the Home Secretary.

It seems that any decisions relating to any statutory duty can be influenced by the authority's availability of resources.

R v Gloucestershire County Council and another ex parte Barry (1997)

This was a House of Lords' decision in respect of the provision of particular services required by statute for disabled persons. The Law Lords said that the cost of such arrangements and its resources were proper considerations for a local authority to take into account when assessing needs and deciding if it is necessary to meet that need.

In respect of police operations the courts have taken note that resources are not infinite and must be allocated between competing requirements. See *R v Chief Constable of Sussex ex parte International Traders' Ferry Ltd* (1997) on page 59.

When a mandatory duty exists by law, it must be undertaken in the light of the financial resources available, but in cases that depend upon the use of discretion, the courts will not interfere with decisions properly made. See also the use of discretionary powers under the heading *ultra vires* doctrine on page 105.

Local policing objectives

Before each financial year, objectives for determining the policing of the area for the year must be determined (section 7). The objectives may be the same objectives as those decided nationally by the Home Secretary (section 37) or can relate to other matters. However, they must be framed to be consistent with the national objectives. Before determining the local policing objectives the authority must:

- consult the chief constable for the area; and
- consider any views obtained as a result of community consultations as described below.

Community consultation

Arrangements must be made by the police authority, after consulting with the chief constable, for obtaining the following information (section 96):

- the views of the people in that area about matters concerning the policing of the area; and
- their co-operation with the police in preventing crime in that area.

The body or person who has the duty of making these arrangements will review the arrangements from time to time to ensure that they are adequate.

Local policing plans

Before each financial year the police authority must issue a plan setting out the proposed arrangements for the policing of the area during the forthcoming year (section 8). This local policing plan must include:

- a statement of the authority's priorities for the year;
- the financial resources expected to be available; and
- how it is proposed to allocate those resources.

The local plan will also give details of the following:

- the national police objectives including any performance targets decided by the Home Secretary (section 38);
- the objectives determined by the police authority itself;
- any performance targets established by the authority itself.

A draft of the local policing plan will be prepared by the chief constable which he then submits to the authority for consideration. If the police authority decides to issue a local policing plan that differs from the draft submitted, the chief constable must be consulted before it is issued.

Rewards for diligence

A police authority may, on the recommendation of the chief constable, grant out of the police fund to members of its police force, rewards for exceptional diligence or other specially meritorious conduct (section 31).

Reporting, etc by police authorities

To the Home Secretary

If required to do so, a police authority must submit a report on any specified matters connected with the policing of its area (section 43).

For general publication

- As soon as possible after the end of each financial year the police authority must issue a report relating to the policing of the authority's area for that year. This report will include an assessment of the extent to which the local policing plan for that year has been carried out (section 9).
- The police authority must arrange for local policing plans (section 8) and annual reports (section 9) to be published appropriately and will also send copies to the Home Secretary.
- Following the receipt of a published inspection report by HM Inspector of Constabulary, the police authority will (section 55):
  o invite the chief constable to comment on the report;
  o prepare its own comments on the report;
  o arrange for the publication of
    . its own comments,
    . the chief constable's comments, and
    . any response by the authority to the chief constable's comments.
- The police authority must arrange for the collection and publication of performance data (Local Government Act 1992). This includes:
  o information on performance standards; and
  o any provisions or recommendations on auditor's reports;
  o any information regarding their police force by the Audit Commission.

Meetings of the police authority

Meetings of the police authority must be open to the public and press but public and press may be excluded during the discussion of confidential information (Local Government Act 1972 as extended by the Local Government (Access to Information) Act 1985). The details of what constitutes 'confidential information' is contained in Schedule 12A of the Act.

Questions on police matters at council meetings

All local councils within the police force area must make arrangements for enabling questions on the discharge of the functions of a police authority to be put by councillors at a meeting arranged for that purpose. The police authority will nominate one or more of its members to attend such a meeting to answer those questions (section 20).

Libel of a police authority

Police authorities, are in the same legal position as any other public authority because, corporately, they cannot be libelled.

Derbyshire County Council v Times Newspapers Ltd and others (1993)

The House of Lords declared that it was contrary to the public interest that organs of government, whether central or local, should have the right to sue for libel because any governmental body should be open to uninhibited public criticism and to allow such actions would place an undesirable fetter on freedom of speech.

Similarly, the elected members could not jointly sue for libel as a political party:

Goldsmith and another v Bhoyrul and others (1997)

It was held in the Queen's Bench Division that it was contrary to the public interest for a political party to have any right at common law to maintain an action for defamation.

However, these judgments would not prevent any individual member of a police authority from pursuing action if he was personally defamed.

Potential causes of conflict

Police forces are controlled by a triumvirate of the police authority, the Home Secretary and the chief constable. The Home Secretary holds the purse strings and has the power of central government behind him whilst the chief constable is responsible for 'operational' matters. The function of the police authority is largely of an administrative nature, which, whilst undoubtedly of great importance, leaves the main levers of power in Whitehall and the chief constable's office.

When a police authority has members of strong political or social views they are sometimes frustrated at their lack of ability to control what is being done by 'their' police force and claim that there is a lack of democratic control over its operations.

Following are examples of police authorities being in conflict with their chief constable and the Home Secretary.

During the miners' strike in 1984 the South Yorkshire Police Authority disagreed with the operational methods being used by their chief constable. To exert more control over him they reportedly removed his power to spend more than £2,000 without the approval of the chairman of the police authority. Such a financial restriction would have had the effect of removing the chief constable's independence. The Attorney General, on behalf of central government, threatened to challenge this decision in the High Court (probably by judicial review). The police authority rescinded the instruction and the matter did not proceed further.

Later in 1984, the miners' strike continuing, the same police authority acted again:

The Force's police horses had been used to control public disorder with considerable effect. The police authority resolved to dispose of its police horses, dispense with half of the police dogs, reduce the force's vehicle fleet and make other cutbacks. The reason given for the resolution was to save £1.6 millions to offset the considerable costs of policing the continuing miners' strike. When he was told about the resolution the Home Secretary claimed that the action was designed to undermine police operations. He also stated that he was prepared to go to the High Court to prevent the resolution being put into effect. As with the earlier incident, the police authority withdrew the resolution and the cuts were not proceeded with.

Two incidents with differing outcomes occurred in Greater Manchester:

The Greater Manchester Police Authority directed Chief Constable Anderton in 1985 to dispose of arms and ammunition that the force had acquired for operational use. After Home Office pressure the instruction was rescinded.

On a later occasion, the same police authority ordered the standing down of the force band as a cost saving measure. During the discussions on this matter it was revealed that many of the musicians were full-time regular police officers. The chief constable objected to this course of action and claimed that the band was of importance to the force. In this case the Home Secretary was not prepared to support the chief constable in his claim and consequently took no action. In due time the economy took effect.

The final example involves a case that did go to court. The Northumbria Police Authority had refused to sanction the acquisition of equipment considered necessary by the chief constable but the equipment was nonetheless supplied to the force on the authority of the Home Secretary. In 1986 the police authority, backed by the Association of Metropolitan Authorities decided to challenge the right of the Home Secretary to veto decisions made by a police authority. The case was initially heard in the High Court who found against the police authority. The case was then appealed to the Court of Appeal and the decision is the leading statement in these matters.

R v Secretary of State for the Home Department ex parte Northumbria Police Authority (1987)

The facts given before the Court of Appeal were that the Home Secretary had issued a Home Office Circular letter setting out a procedure whereby a chief constable could obtain plastic baton rounds and CS gas equipment despite the absence of the police authority's approval. The authority claimed that this arrangement was *ultra vires* the Home Secretary's powers.

The court held that the Crown has prerogative power to keep the peace, which was bound up with its undoubted right to see that crime was prevented and justice administered. The Crown could not act under the prerogative if to do so would be incompatible with statute. However, the statutory right of a police authority to provide equipment was not a monopoly and supply of the equipment by the Crown under prerogative power was not inconsistent with the police authority's powers.

The words of section 4 Police Act 1964 under which this action was initiated were subsequently amended. The equivalent powers are now under section 6, see page 64.

A police authority can give the chief constable advice on administrative matters, but it seems doubtful if the authority is empowered to give any instructions outside the administrative sphere.

However, a definitive statement on this matter awaits the time when a police authority gives a chief constable an instruction that he construes as being 'operational' and consequently refuses to obey it. Then, only if the police authority sought a judicial review seeking to make the chief constable obey the instruction as part of his public duty, might a definitive statement be made.

7 National Service Authorities

The establishment of National Service Authorities

Although the National Criminal Intelligence Service and the National Crime Squad existed prior to 1997, the Police Act 1997 placed them on a statutory footing. The Act established the principle of National Service Authorities as corporate bodies modelled on the structure and function of provincial police authorities.

The two authorities established by the Police Act 1997 are National Criminal Intelligence Service (NCIS) Authority and National Crime Squad (NCS) Authority (sections 1 and 47, Schedules 1 and 2 PA 1997). Their structures are not identical, but broadly speaking, they follow the pattern described below.

The Authorities are responsible respectively for maintaining and ensuring the efficient and effective performances of the NCIS and the NCS (sections 2, 3 and 48, 49 PA 1997), see page 29 *et seq*.

Membership of the Authorities

The members of each Authority consist of (Schedules 1 and 2 PA 1997):
- independent members appointed by the Home Secretary;
- representatives of chief police officers;
- representatives of police authorities; and
- one representative from the Home Office.

The Chairman must be one of the independent members.

Appointments by the Authorities

The Authority, subject to the approval of the Home Secretary, is responsible for the appointment and removal of the Director General (sections 6, 7 and 52, 53 PA 1997). He holds the rank of chief constable and his relationship with the Service Authority is similar to the relationship of a provincial chief constable with his police authority.

A Clerk to the Authority must be appointed (sections 14 and 59 PA 1997) and other officers and employees may be appointed to enable the discharge of the Authority's functions (sections 13, 15 and 58, 60 PA 1997).

Functions of the Authorities

Consultation

National service authorities will, after consulting their Director General, make arrangements for obtaining the views of (sections 41 and 85 PA 1997):

- the police authorities responsible for maintaining UK police forces;
- the NCIS/NCS Service Authority as appropriate;
- the Commissioners of Customs and Excise; and
- any other appropriate body;

about the Authority and the NCIS/NCS as appropriate.

Objectives and performance targets

Before each financial year the objectives for the forthcoming year will be determined after due consultation. The objectives may be the same as those determined by the Home Secretary (see page 76) or may relate to other consistent matters (sections 3 and 49 PA 1997)

When performing its functions a national authority must pay due regard to (sections 2 and 48 PA 1997):

- any objectives determined for the NCIS/NCS by the Home Secretary;
- the annual objectives determined by the authority itself;
- any performance targets established by the Home Secretary (sections 27 and 71 PA 1997) or by the authority itself; and
- the annual service plan issued by the authority itself.

Discipline and complaints

The members of the Service Authority must keep themselves informed as to the operation of established complaints and disciplinary procedures within the organisation (sections 40 and 84 PA 1997).

Reports

Service plan

Draft service plans will be submitted to the Authority by their Director General, see page 31. The Authority will arrange for its publication, but if the published plan differs from that submitted by the Director General he will be consulted before its publication (sections 4 and 50 PA 1997).

Annual report

At the end of each financial year each authority will prepare a report on the performance of its organisation during the year (sections 5 and 51 PA 1997). The report will include an assessment of the extent to which the service plan for that year has been met.

Publication

Service plans and annual reports will be published and copies will be sent to the following:

- the Home Secretary;
- each police authority and national service authority;
- all chief constables and directors general;
- the Commissioners of Customs and Excise;
- other relevant authorities.

Finance

The Authority must keep a fund to be known as the service fund (sections 16 and 61 PA 1997). All receipts and expenditure to and from the Authority must be paid from this fund and full accounts must be kept of all transactions.

See further details in Chapter 9.

8 Secretary of State for the Home Department

The office of Home Secretary

The Home Secretary deals with all of those internal affairs in England and Wales that have not been assigned to other government departments. He is concerned with a wide range of responsibilities, being especially concerned with the administration of justice, public order, criminal law and supervision of the Security Service.

He is, personally, the link between the Queen and the general public. As such he exercises certain prerogative powers on her behalf, including that of maintaining the Queen's peace and the policing activities that are associated with it.

The Home Secretary is the police authority for the Metropolitan Police, but he has no direct responsibility for the operations of provincial police forces in England and Wales or for the National Criminal Intelligence Service or the National Crime Squad. The legal control over these bodies lies with the police and national authorities, however, the Police Acts give him many powers that he exercises over them.

Duties of the Home Secretary in relation to provincial police forces and national services

The Home Secretary must exercise his powers under the Police Acts in a way that is calculated to promote the efficiency and effectiveness of the police (section 36 and sections 25 and 70 PA 1997).

Alteration of police force areas

The Home Secretary may make alterations to specific police areas in England and Wales (except the City of London). The making of any such alteration must follow the laid down procedures (sections 32, 33 and 34), see page 8.

Appointment and removal of chief officers of police

The appointment of the chief officers by a police or national authority is subject to the approval of the Home Secretary (sections 11 and 12 and sections 6 and 52 PA 1997). The short list of candidates drawn up before an appointment must also be approved by the Home Secretary. Chief officers are chief constables, assistant chief constables and Directors General of the national services.

The Home Secretary may require a police or national authority to exercise their power to call upon a chief officer to retire in the interests of efficiency or effectiveness (section 42 and sections 29 and 74 PA 1997).

Setting of objectives for police and national service authorities

The Home Secretary may determine objectives for the policing of all police areas/organisations (section 37 and sections 26 and 71 PA 1997), but before making an order in this matter he will consult:

- persons whom he considers to represent the interests of police authorities;
- persons whom he considers to represent the interests of chief constables; and
- in the cases of the NCIS and NCS, their respective Service Authorities.

A statutory instrument containing an order describing the objectives must be laid before Parliament after being made.

Setting of performance targets

Where an objective has been determined as above, the Home Secretary may direct police authorities to establish levels of performance ('performance targets') to be aimed at in seeking to achieve the objective (section 38 and sections 27 and 72 PA 1997).

- All authorities or some particular authorities may be directed to achieve particular performance targets.
- The direction might impose conditions with which the performance targets must conform.
- Different authorities might have different conditions imposed.

Codes of practice

The Home Secretary may issue codes of practice relating to the functions of police and service authorities, eg to govern financial relationships between a police authority and its police force (section 39 and sections 28, 73 and 101 PA 1997).

Power to give directions to authorities after adverse reports

The Home Secretary may at any time require the inspectors of constabulary to carry out an inspection of any police force or service and when an inspection report states:

- that in the opinion of the HM Inspector of Constabulary, the force or service inspected is not efficient or not effective; **or**
- that unless remedial measures are taken, the force will cease to be efficient or effective,

   the Home Secretary may then direct the police or service authority to:
   - take specified measures to rectify the situation (section 40 and sections 30 and 75 PA 1997); and
   - allocate a specified minimum amount of the police budget (section 41).

Inquiries into policing matters

The Home Secretary may cause a local inquiry to be held by a person appointed by him into any matter connected with the policing of any area or concerning the NCIS or NCS. The inquiry may be held in public or in private as the Home Secretary may direct (section 49 and sections 34 and 79 PA 1997).

The appointed chairman of such a local inquiry may, by summons, require any person to attend and give evidence, including the production of any documents. Evidence can be taken on oath. It is an offence for anyone summonsed to refuse or fail to attend or to falsify any document (section 250 Local Government Act 1972 and sections 34 and 79 PA 1997).

If the report of the inquiry is not published, a summary of its findings and conclusions shall be made known so far as is consistent with the public interest (section 49 and sections 34 and 79 PA 1997).

Reports, etc on policing matters

Reports from police and national service authorities

When required, an authority must submit a report on any specified matters connected with the discharge of the authority's functions in respect of its own policing responsibilities (section 43 and sections 31 and 76 PA 1997).

Reports from chief constables and directors general

Chief constables and directors general will submit reports to the Home Secretary:

- on such specified matters connected with the policing of his area (section 44 and sections 32 and 77 PA 1997);
- at the end of each financial year, a copy of the chief constable's report to his police authority (section 44 and sections 32 and 77 PA 1997);
- particulars of offences, offenders, criminal proceedings and the state of crime in his police area. These statistics will be collated and laid before Parliament by the Home Secretary (section 45 and sections 33 and 78 PA 1997).

Reports from the Police Complaints Authority

The Police Complaints Authority will carry out research and report to the Home Secretary:

- on any matters specified by the Home Secretary;
- on matters coming to the notice of the PCA which the members consider appropriate by reason of their gravity or other exceptional circumstances.

Copies of any of the above reports will also be sent to the authority and/or chief constable concerned (section 79).

An annual report will be submitted detailing the discharge of the PCA's functions during the year. The Home Secretary will lay the report before parliament and copies of it will be sent to each police authority together with any supporting statistical or other information (section 79).

Home Office Circulars

Home Office Circulars are letters sent to chief constables and police/service authorities although those that relate to sensitive operational or security matters are restricted to chief constables and directors general. The circulars do not have any legal authority being formally described as suggestions and not directions. However, any prudent chief constable will not forget who is doing the suggesting.

Finance

The Home Secretary makes financial grants to police authorities. For each financial year the Home Secretary, in consultation with the Treasury, determines:

- the aggregate amount of grants to be made to all police forces; and
- the amount of the grant to be made to each police authority.

He will then prepare a report setting out the considerations taken into account in deciding the allocations (section 46). In addition grants may be made for capital expenditure incurred, or to be incurred, for police purposes (section 47).

The NCIS and NCS are funded by a levy made on police forces. The Home Secretary will order the calculation, setting, collection, administration and payment of the levies (sections 17 and 62 PA 1997).

See Chapter 9 for further details on finance.

Regulations for the governance of police forces

General regulations

The Home Secretary may make regulations as to the government, administration and conditions of service of police forces (section 50).

Regulations can be made concerning the following matters:

- the ranks to be held by members of police forces;
- the qualifications for appointment and promotion of members of police forces;
- periods of service on probation;
- voluntary retirement of members of police forces;
- the conduct, efficiency and effectiveness of members of police forces and the maintenance of discipline;
- the suspension of members of a police force from membership of that force and from their office as constable;
- the maintenance of personal records of members of police forces;
- the duties which are or are not to be performed by members of police forces;
- the treatment as occasions of police duty of attendance at meetings of the Police Federations and of any similar body recognised by the Home Secretary;

- the hours of duty, leave, pay and allowances of members of police forces; and
- the issue, use and return of police clothing, personal equipment and accoutrements.

Police Federation regulations

The Home Secretary can make regulations prescribing the constitution, proceedings, membership, funding, etc of Police Federations (section 60).

Disciplinary procedure regulations

Regulations can also be made to establish procedures, for cases in which a member of a police force may be dealt with by (section 50):
- dismissal;
- requirement to resign;
- reduction in rank;
- reduction in rate of pay;
- fine;
- reprimand;
- caution; and
- regulations governing the disciplining of chief and assistant chief constables by their police authority.

The Home Secretary may make regulations regarding the discipline procedures to be followed in police forces and by the Police Complaints Authority (sections 81 and 82 and sections 37, 39, 81 and 83 PA 1997).

Discipline guidance notes

The Home Secretary can issue guidance to police authorities, chief constables and other members of police forces concerning the discharge of their discipline functions (sections 83 and 87).

Special constables regulations

The Home Secretary may make regulations as to the government, administration and conditions of service of special constables concerning the following matters (section 51):
- the qualifications for appointment of special constable;
- the retirement of special constables;
- the suspension of special constables from their office as constable;
- the allowances payable to special constables;
- the application to special constables, of any provisions relating to the payment of pensions.

Police cadets regulations

The Home Secretary may make regulations as to the government, administration and conditions of service of police cadets (section 52).

Standard of equipment regulations

The Home Secretary may make regulations requiring equipment provided or used for police purposes to satisfy such requirements as to design and performance as may be prescribed in the regulations (section 53 and sections 35 and 80 PA 1997).

Common services regulations

The Home Secretary may make regulations requiring all police forces to use specified services or facilities or services of a specified description (section 36 PA 1997).

The Security Service

The Home Secretary is responsible for the Security Service including the appointment of the Director General (sections 1 and 2 SS Act). The Director General must make an annual report on the work of the Security Service to the Prime Minister and the Home Secretary, and may at any other time report to either of them (section 2 SS Act). See page 35 *et seq* for further details.

Part III

An overview of the financing of provincial police forces

9   Financing of Police Forces

No two provincial police authorities have identical financial arrangements as elements of both income and expenditure vary in accordance with local conditions. This chapter describes in general terms how police financing operates but probably no single force's arrangements will follow the descriptions in detail. All figures are approximations.

The police fund

It is the duty of a police authority to maintain a police fund (section 14). All receipts must be paid into the fund, all expenditures shall be paid out of the fund and accounts must be kept of the fund's transactions. A police authority is also authorised to raise and spend money for acquiring capital assets.

Police authorities are permitted to supply goods and services to any person (section 18 Local Authorities (Goods and Services) Act 1970).

All of the financial transactions of the police fund and any borrowing of funds are controlled by financial regulations approved by the Home Secretary. Financial supervision is undertaken by HM Inspectorate of Constabulary and the Audit Commission.

Form of accounts

Following normal accounting practice police authority expenditure is divided into two parts:

Revenue expenditure (also called **current expenditure**)
This consists of the spending on goods and services, including staff wages and pensions, which are needed to keep the organisation working on a day-by-day basis. The items concerned are said to he 'consumable' or not long lasting. For convenience, minor capital items costing up to a few thousand pounds will be paid for from the current expenditure account.

Capital expenditure
This is the money spent upon those things that are permanent or semi-permanent, and will be used over and over, these things are called 'fixed assets'. Examples of capital items are buildings, communication systems, vehicles and other expensive items. When large sums of money are borrowed to pay for new fixed assets, the debt is 'serviced' from the current account. (To service a debt means to pay off the sum borrowed by instalments together with the amount of interest that is charged by the lender.)

Sources of funding for revenue expenditure

Each police authority holds its own financial reserves, sets its own budget and receives the following monies:

- the specific police grant (Home Office);
- any additional grants in connection with safeguarding national security (Home Office);
- a contribution from the revenue support grants (RSG) for the local government areas policed by the force (Department of the Environment);
- a contribution from the non-domestic rates payers (the uniform business rate (UBR)) (Department of the Environment);
- a contribution from local council tax payers (District Billing Authorities).

Police authority sources of funding

The approximate portions of income from the various sources are:

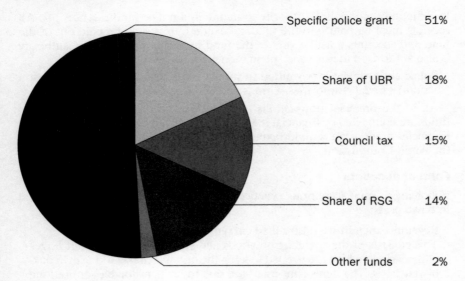

Specific police grant	51%
Share of UBR	18%
Council tax	15%
Share of RSG	14%
Other funds	2%

The proportions shown are approximations as they vary from force to force

Other, additional funds will be available from all or some of the following:

- special grants from individual local authorities;
- income earned from various police activities;
- investment income;
- gifts or loans of money or other property, including commercial sponsorship, in connection with the discharge of any of the authority's functions.

Central government funding for revenue expenditure

The formula for distribution of funds

Before 1994 funds were allocated to each police force on an *ad hoc* basis but it was felt that this was not a suitable way to disburse public money.

In that year it was decided that a global sum should be allocated to the police service and this money would then be divided between the forces. To this end a formula (section 46) was devised to measure each force's workload in terms of:

- the likely number of police incidents to be dealt with during the year;
- the extent of crime and the type of housing in the police area;
- the amount of traffic based on the population and extent of motorways in the police area;
- the incidence of public disorder recorded in the police area;
- the management of community policing.

Additionally, the following 'non-workload' factors were included in the formula:

- police establishment expenditure;
- pensions expenditure;
- any particular security related expenditure.

There are many components included under each of these headings and when taken together they provide a numerical value that can be used to determine the relative needs of each police force. The grant 'cake' is then divided according to relative need.

The details of the formula have been altered year on year but the basic principle has remained unchanged.

The specific police grant

The aggregate annual grant payable to all forces in England and Wales is decided by the Home Secretary with the agreement of the Chancellor of the Exchequer (section 46).

The aggregate sum available is then divided proportionately between forces according to their needs as assessed by the formula. This ensures that all forces are treated equitably and that the grant is shared according to the needs identified (section 46).

Safeguarding national security

The Home Secretary may make grants to police forces to cover any expenditure incurred in connection with safeguarding national security (section 48).

Other public funding

The police standard spending assessment (PSSA) is the government's estimate of what a police authority should spend to achieve a standard level of service provision. It is assessed by using the formula mentioned above, the specific police grant is subtracted and the sum remaining is called the PSSA. Funds to cover the PSSA are provided from the revenue support grant, the uniform business rate and by precepting on the council tax.

Preception

Police authorities will precept on the constituent district councils of its police area for that proportion of its budget that has to be met by the council tax (CT) payers of the police area. As illustrated below, the district councils collect money on behalf of their local police authority, but they have no direct influence on the amount that is collected.

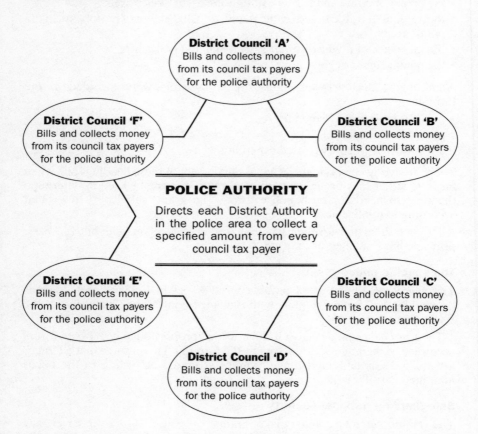

When a police authority discusses precepting decisions, there must be (section 19):

• at least half of the members of the police authority in attendance when decisions are made; and
• more than half of those present must be local council appointed members.

The Home Secretary can, after receiving an adverse inspection report on a police force, direct that the annual budget of the police authority for any financial year must be greater than a specified minimum amount (section 41). Any precept that is inconsistent with such a direction will be void (section 41). Failure to precept to meet the specified minimum standard would be a suitable matter for judicial review.

Precepted expenditure counts as expenditure for the police authority not the constituent local councils for capping purposes.

Local council grants

Local councils can make grants to their local police authority either unconditionally or subject to particular conditions that are agreed with the chief constable (section 92).

The local council must not exceed its own capping level when providing such a grant but the additional funding could be over the police authority's capping level.

Non-public funding of police services

Acceptance of gifts, loans and sponsorship

Police authorities can accept gifts of money and gifts or loans of other property on appropriate terms, including commercial sponsorship (section 93). To this end the Home Secretary has agreed to allow police forces to raise up to one per cent of their annual budget in commercial sponsorship deals.

A variety of such deals have been reported in the press such as the provision of motor vehicles, for non-operational purposes, carrying commercial logos.

Provision of special paid services

Police have a common law duty (see wording of attestation) to protect persons and their property against reasonably apprehended violence, etc and therefore, a police authority cannot impose a charge for supplying extra protection to persons in need of it. However, if the 'special' duty requested goes beyond the normal public provision then it is outside the scope of that common law duty. In such cases the chief constable is empowered to provide special police services within his police area, subject to the payment for the services rendered (section 25).

A major requirement for special services is in relation to football matches and other sporting events. The football clubs have resented the amount that has to be paid and in 1987 sought a legal ruling in the matter.

Harris v Sheffield United Football Club Ltd (1987)

It was claimed that as the chief constable had been of the opinion that the attendance of police officers at the football ground had been necessary for the maintenance of law and order and the protection of life and property the club should not be liable to make any payment as the police were merely carrying out their public duty.

Held: The provision of police officers, by calling on officers who would otherwise have been off-duty, to attend regularly at football matches at the ground of a football club in order to deal with the possibility of violence constituted the provision of special police services for which the police authority was entitled to make a charge and recover payment from the club.

In the present financial climate a variety of schemes have been put forward by different chief constables to gain funds from the sale of police expertise and authority as special services. There is nothing new in this approach, for instance, from 1946 until the late 1960s Birkenhead Borough Police used to provide police officers for 'cargo supervision' in the Birkenhead Docks' sheds. The officers deployed on this duty worked inside the dock sheds with the function of preventing cargo theft. The cost of the officers thus engaged was borne by the Mersey Docks and Harbour Board as a special service quite separate and apart from the normal policing of the Docks.

Factors affecting revenue expenditure

Personnel costs

Labour costs (including pensions) are roughly 80% of a total police force budget, the remaining 20% has to cover the cost of non-human resources. This means that the budget for 'hardware' is relatively small with little room for manoeuvre by financial managers.

The salaries and pensions of police officers are agreed nationally so any increase in these payments will alter the proportions of the budget accordingly. For instance, assume that the overall budget has been fixed. An unbudgeted 5% increase in personnel costs would raise the personnel proportion from 80% to 84% and the operational proportion would decline from 20% to 16% – down by a quarter.

With the stringent financial controls now required in the public sector, all forces must examine personnel costs closely. This means controlling factors such as overtime payments, new recruitment and so on. Some factors are not always fully appreciated, for example, in providing continuous 24 hour cover on a single beat it is not enough to say that three police officers each working an eight hour shift is adequate. Every officer will have two rest days per week, annual leave, periods of training and probably some time off for sickness and/or injury during the year. This means that the number of personnel required to maintain full 24 hour coverage is at least five officers per individual beat. If police forces only operated during normal business hours they would be much cheaper to run!

Financial gearing

Even if the police authority is authorised to exceed the PSSA there will be difficulties in obtaining much greater funds from local council tax-payers. Just under 15% of revenue spending will come from the precept, therefore to increase total spending by 1% would need about a 6–7% increase in the precepted part of the council tax.

The diagram below illustrates how much the 'slice' has to be increased to make a significant difference to the size of the whole cake.

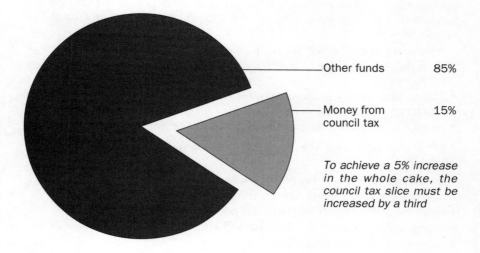

Other funds   85%

Money from   15%
council tax

To achieve a 5% increase in the whole cake, the council tax slice must be increased by a third

Cash limits

All local authorities, including police authorities, are subjected to cash limits by central government.

This means that when the PSSA has been decided it includes funds to cover the government's estimates of:

- potential inflation;
- probable pay increases;
- fuel price rises; and
- other likely increases in costs;

that might occur during the next financial year. Central government will not provide additional supplementary grants to police authorities if there are rises in costs which exceed the estimates.

If there are any such increases during the financial year they will have to be dealt with by the police authority without any additional government funding.

Capping

Even if a police authority decides that more money is needed than has been allocated in the PSSA, it is unlikely that they will be able to precept any greater amount. Spending will probably be 'capped' at that limit, but note that local councils are still empowered to give additional grants providing they don't breach their own capping limits (section 92).

Police force revenue expenditure budgets

The main purpose of a budget is to decide how the money received during the year should be spent. Preparing a budget gives an opportunity to review the services that are furnished and the ways in which they are provided. The budget should:

- represent a plan of action for the forthcoming year;
- show the financial effects of different policy options and thus ensure 'value for money';
- ensure that money is spent only for the purposes for which it has been provided;
- provide a 'yardstick' to measure administrative performance.

At the time of setting the budget the following matters will need to be considered:

- the effects on prices of the anticipated level of inflation;
- new or expanded commitments arising as a result of new legislation;
- changing requirements for particular policing activities;
- changing demographic patterns that will affect policing;
- changes to central service charges;
- changes to income.

After due consideration the budget for revenue expenditure will be devised to cover all of the resources that the force needs in order to operate efficiently.

Emergencies

Normally, once the budget has been approved, no alterations are permitted; even inflationary increases in prices have to be paid for from the budget as it stands. However, cases may arise when additional money must be spent to cover unforeseen problems that have to be dealt with. Examples of such emergencies are natural or man-made disasters that affect large numbers of people in the police area and serious ongoing public disorder.

The chief constable will have a small contingency fund at his disposal to meet some emergencies, but this will be for a relatively small sum of money when compared with the total spending for the year. Using this fund would keep the force's total current expenditure budget at the same level.

Approval might be sought from the police authority for a supplementary budget. The police authority will consider the application and may need to seek either a supplementary grant from central government or permission to borrow money. This, if approved, will give the force additional funds to meet the emergency. However, if the money was raised by borrowing, the cost will be felt in future years when the additional loans have to be serviced.

Capital expenditure

Capital expenditure over £1 million requires Home Office approval. Advice in respect of capital projects will be offered to the Home Secretary by the police authority, the chief constable and HM Inspector of Constabulary.

Capital projects will be considered, taking into account the following factors:

- the effects upon the efficiency of the force of having/not having the capital item;
- the potential effects upon the general public;
- the cost relative to the possible benefits that may be gained;
- the effect on the police authority's burden of debt servicing;
- the central government's current policies regarding public sector financing.

When a capital project has been approved, a grant may be provided by the Home Secretary to cover all or part of the expenditure (section 47). Additional cash beyond any grant has to be raised by the police authority who will be given permission to borrow the necessary funds. These loans will subsequently be serviced through revenue expenditure.

It is probable that approval may be given for small items of capital expenditure to be made via the revenue account.

National Service Authorities

The NCIS and the NCS must maintain a service fund (sections 16 and 61 PA 1997) which is similar in its operation to the police fund see page 83.

The monies needed are raised from the police forces that are served by means of an annual levy. The Home Secretary will calculate, set, collect, administer and arrange the payment of the levies from police authorities to the service authorities (sections 17 and 62 PA 1997).

Both the NCIS and NCS are empowered to make charges for their services and accept gifts, loans or commercial sponsorship in a similar way to that authorised for police forces (sections 19, 20, 24 and 64, 65, 69 PA 1997), see pages 87–89.

Part IV

The institutional authorities that exercise
supervision over policing activities

10 Her Majesty's Inspectors of Constabulary

Appointment

HM Inspectors of Constabulary (HMIC) are appointed by the Home Secretary on behalf of Her Majesty the Queen. One HMIC is appointed as the chief inspector of constabulary (HMCIC) (section 54).

The first appointment of HMIC occurred in 1856 to coincide with the authorised payment of a police grant by central government. The role of the inspectorate has been enhanced in recent years and has been the means of centralising and co-ordinating standards and methods throughout the country.

To undertake the greater amount of supervisory work involved the Home Secretary is empowered to appoint assistant inspectors of constabulary and police staff officers (section 56). The Home Secretary has also taken the step of appointing non-police HMIC to gain the benefit of their specialist knowledge.

Supervising duties of the inspectorate

It is the duty of HMIC to inspect and report to the Home Secretary on the efficiency and effectiveness of every police force in England and Wales (section 54).

For many years the office of HMIC was something of a sinecure calling for no great effort on the part of individual inspectors. As recently as the 1950/60s the annual inspection of a police force presented more of an outward form of supervision than an investigative review of a force's activities during the year. Members of the inspected force were drawn up in a military style parade and HMIC asked non-demanding questions of those present. A variety of reports and documents, updated, but otherwise little different to the previous year's papers were produced and taken away by the inspector. Sometimes the chief constable would raise issues with HMIC who would then take them up with the police authority. Assuming the police authority 'played ball' the certificate of efficiency was signed and the HMIC could be more or less forgotten until the next year.

Since 1984 the pattern has changed considerably and inspections are now really designed to investigate the efficiency of a police force's operations. Before the inspection HMIC's staff officers visit the force to gather information and report to him about the force's activities or arrangements in particular areas. HMIC examines the staff officers' reports before visiting the force and is thus able to concentrate his inspection in those areas he feels to be most appropriate.

In 1987 a complex computer-based management information system, the Matrix of Police Indicators, was brought into use. This system involves the collation of a lot of data from police forces in a standardised way. The resulting information permits HMIC to inspect all forces in a standardised pattern, using best practice benchmarks as the means of evaluation. This process is, in effect, being used to shape national police activity into a common, government determined, pattern.

Every force is inspected at least once per year, the inspections being of two types:

• full primary inspections which are designed to cover most areas of the force's activities and its organisational structure which are undertaken every third year;

• performance review inspections which are limited to specific aspects of policing by investigating in greater depth some of the areas covered by the performance targets determined by the Home Secretary (section 38).

Additionally, thematic inspections are undertaken which cover a single issue such as equal opportunities within police forces.

Certificate of efficiency

Following the annual inspection of a police force a certificate of efficiency will be issued if the force merits it. In the past this was a prerequisite before the payment of the government police grant to each police force and in earlier years the grant was either withheld or reduced for those forces not considered to be efficient.

Nowadays it would not be politically desirable to punish a non-efficient force by such a drastic step as it would make a bad situation even worse, and the larger police areas would mean that far more people would be affected by an underfunded police force.

The Home Secretary is empowered to direct that remedial measures be undertaken by the police authority (section 40) or for the police budget to be set at a specified minimum level (section 41). During the mid-1990s Derbyshire Constabulary, after adverse reports, was refused a certificate of efficiency for three successive years. The Derbyshire Police Authority was required to improve the funding arrangements for the force.

The performance targets set by the Home Secretary (section 38) can be directed at particular police authorities and may have conditions attached that must be obeyed. This power could no doubt be used in the case of any police force receiving a conditional certificate of efficiency or not receiving the certificate at all. If a police authority did not obey such a direction the Home Secretary would be able to seek the imposition of sanctions through the courts.

Complaints and discipline

HM Inspectors must keep themselves informed as to the working of the complaints and discipline procedures within the forces that they are inspecting (section 77 and section 40 PA 1997).

Reports

Inspection reports

Following the inspection of a police force HMIC will report to the Home Secretary on its efficiency and effectiveness (section 54). The Home Secretary will arrange for this report to be published subject to the exclusion of any material that would be against national security interests or anything that might jeopardise the safety of any person (section 55).

The Home Secretary will send copies of the published report to the police authority and chief constable of the concerned force. The police authority will (section 55):

- invite the chief constable to submit comments on the published report;
- prepare its own comments on the report;
- and will arrange for the publication of:
  - its own comments;
  - the chief constable's comments; and
  - any response by the police authority to the chief constable's comments.

A copy of this document must be sent to the Home Secretary.

National services

The National Criminal Intelligence Service and the National Crime Squad are both subject to HMIC inspection as appropriate and the Home Secretary may at any time require HMIC to inspect them (sections 30 and 75 PA 1997).

If, following an inspection of either of these bodies, the inspector's report indicates that the NCIS/NCS is not efficient or effective, or that some remedial measures should be taken, the appropriate service authority can be directed to take specified measures to rectify the situation.

Annual report by HM Chief Inspector of Constabulary

The HMCIC must submit an annual report to the Home Secretary on the findings of the inspectorate during the year. A copy of this report must be laid before Parliament (section 54).

Other reports

Any HMIC may be required to carry out additional duties for the purpose of furthering police efficiency and effectiveness as directed by the Home Secretary, reporting accordingly (section 54).

11 The Audit Commission

The establishment of the Audit Commission

The Local Government Finance Act 1982 created the Audit Commission. The Commission has 15 members appointed by the government being drawn from industry, local government and trade unions. The intended purpose of the Commission is to increase the independence of audit and to increase the efficiency approach to local finances.

The Audit Commission appoints auditors to inspect the accounts of local authorities, including police authorities. Additionally, it is specifically charged with promoting more value for money (VFM) auditing.

In its mission statement (1993) it declares:

> The Audit Commission promotes proper stewardship of public finances and helps those responsible for the management and delivery of public services to achieve economy, efficiency and effectiveness. It aims to be a 'driving force in the improvement of public services' which it seeks to achieve through auditing public service accounts to ensure their probity and regularity and producing national studies of value for money.

The Commission produces regular VFM studies (numbering several thousand), together with performance indicators and comparisons. Its reports cover all aspects of local government housing, management, vehicle maintenance, parks, policies, education, etc and its various VFM studies have identified savings by local authorities amounting to about £2 billion per year.

One of the earliest of these reports that affected the police service called 'Footing The Bill: Financing Provincial Police Forces' criticised the existing financial systems in the police service which it claimed:

> ... do not promote the economic, efficient and effective use of resources.

A later report, entitled 'Effective Policing – Performance Review in Police Forces', concluded:

> The management style in the police service should be governed by the fact that its officers are all professionals who should be delegated responsibility for taking decisions and using their own initiative, harnessing their policing experience and knowledge of their local communities. The counterbalance to this is that officers should be held accountable for their actions through a performance review mechanism. The police service has made considerable progress in this direction in recent years but there is much that needs to be done, and many improvements can be put in train within a short time. It is essential:

- that the emphasis is on adoption of an appropriate management culture, directing and enabling high performance by individuals, instead of on detailed styles of management systems which may obscure the principles involved;
- that output-based, quantifiable performance indicators are developed by police forces, acting on guidance from the Home Office and HMIC, and in discussion with their police authorities; and
- that the growing public debate about the quality and future of the police service is informed by a better understanding of what police forces do, how they do it, and what they do it with.

Under all of these headings, concerted action is required by the government, by police authorities and by chief constables and the officers under them, if the police service is to rise to the challenges before it.

In July 1991, Prime Minister Major announced new rights for all citizens in respect of their usage of public services. This Citizen's Charter includes police forces and it states:

All police forces should deliver standards of service which go as far as possible to meet the expectations of the public.

Performance indicators

Performance indicators are used to assess the effectiveness of police activity in particular areas expressed in terms of public satisfaction with the:
- police response to emergency calls;
- service provided at police stations;
- initial response to victims of violent crime;
- initial response to victims of dwelling house burglary;
- service to victims at the scene of road accidents;
- level of police foot and mobile patrols.

The outlines of suitable indicators designed to make a quantitative assessment of the detailed activities that go towards assessing matters are devised by the ACPO, HM Inspectorate of Constabulary and the Audit Commission. Each year the list of indicators is extended and there are nearly 40 of them now in being.

Using the outlines, individual forces devise their own performance specifications that take into account its own particular circumstances. However, all forces follow broadly similar measurements for their own individual performance indicators.

Examples of the quantitative indicators used include:
- recorded crimes per 1,000 population;
- percentage of crimes cleared up by primary means;
- percentage of violent crimes cleared up by primary means;
- percentage of burglaries in houses and flats cleared up by primary means;

- crimes cleared up by primary means per officer;
- officers available for ordinary duty per 1,000 population;
- proportion of uniformed officers' time spent in public;
- expenditure on policing per head of population; and
- 999 calls and immediate response, incident target times and performance.

The standards attained by police forces are monitored by the Audit Commission, who, at the end of each year publishes *Local Authority Performance Indicators: Police*. This publication provides tables illustrating the comparative performance of all English and Welsh Forces. However, the main purpose of these data is not to compare one force with another, especially were policing conditions are very different, but to compare the performance of each force with itself in successive years.

Police authorities are required to collect and publish their own performance data and any other relevant information published by the Audit Commission together with Auditor's reports or recommendations (Local Government Act 1992).

It is worth recording that Paul Vevers, director of Audit Support at the Audit Commission having overall responsibility for the police performance indicators was reported as saying (*Police Review*, 31 January 1997):

As our annual consultation exercise with the service has revealed, a lot more still needs to be done to broaden out the indicators to cover the harder-to-measure areas of policing and to ensure that performance is measured consistently by forces.

The statesmanlike way in which the service has increasingly accepted the principle of publishing details of performance provides a very positive backdrop against which such further development can take place.

Audit Commission publications

Several support and advisory papers have been published by the Audit Commission since 1988 covering a variety of police activities. They are produced following in-depth reviews in representative police forces. The papers are intended to illustrate best practices and obtaining value for money in the deployment of police resources. Following is a list of Police Papers produced to date:

Administrative Support for Operational Police Officers	1988
Improving the Performance of the Fingerprint Service	1988
Improving Vehicle Fleet Management in the Police Service	1989
The Management of Police Training	1989
Calling all Forces: Improving Police Communications Rooms	1990
Footing the Bill: Financing Provincial Police Forces	1990
Taking Care of the Coppers: Income Generation by Provincial Police Forces	1990

Effective Policing: Performance Review in Police Forces	1990
Reviewing the Organisation of Provincial Police Forces	1991
Pounds and Coppers: Financial Delegation in Provincial Police Forces	1991
Fine Lines: Improving the Traffic Warden Service	1992
Helping with Enquiries: Tackling Crime Effectively	1993
Cheques and Balances: A Management Handbook on Police Planning and Financial Delegation	1994
Cheques and Balances: A Framework for Improving Police Accountability Executive Briefing	1994
Tackling Crime Effectively: Management Handbook	1994
Streetwise: Effective Police Patrol	1996
Tackling Patrol Effectively: Management Handbook	1996

In addition to the foregoing, several audit guides relating to police accounts have also been published.

An examination of the range of topics covered shows that Audit Commission reviews of police activities are overlapping the supervisory functions of HM Inspectorate of Constabulary. In the opinion of some commentators this overlap leads to the conclusion that all functions should be subsumed into one organisation or the apparent lack of demarcation could lead to conflict between the two bodies.

12 Control by the Judiciary

The scope of judicial review

There is a general principle of English law that statutory powers and duties must be exercised with reasonable care so as to prevent the occurrence of reasonably foreseeable damage to private rights or unnecessary aggravation of any damage that is necessarily caused for the general public benefit. These matters are part of administrative law that is notorious for its complexity.

With the notable exception of actions taken under the authority of the royal prerogative, all public bodies are creatures of statute. This means that the actions of the Home Office, police authorities, chief constables and the members of their forces are defined within the statutes that create and control them.

The judiciary has always jealously guarded the principle that only they can interpret the law and therefore define the limits of any statutory authority. It follows that the High Court can examine the administrative actions of any public body to ensure that the action is carried out within the terms of the law. The constitutional reason for this judicial power is the simple fact that no executive body should be allowed to be the final judge of its own powers.

The legal procedures involved in seeking judicial review are contained in the Rules of the Supreme Court 1965, Order 53.

In any contentious issue the High Court may make an authoritative statement of the law in the matter and that precedent remains unless and until Parliament enacts a contrary statute. However, it must be emphasised that the High Court does not decide whether a particular administrative act is right or wrong but only whether it is legal or not as was emphasised in the following case:

Chief Constable of the North Wales Police v Evans (1982)

This case related to the dismissal of a probationer constable who sought reinstatement in the force. Lord Hailsham, the Lord Chancellor, gave his learned opinion about the proper scope of the remedy of judicial review in the following terms:

1 Judicial review was intended to protect individuals against abuse of power by many authorities. It was not intended to take away from those authorities the powers and discretions properly vested in them by law. It was intended to see that the relevant authorities used their powers properly.

2 The purpose of the remedy was to ensure the authority gave the individual fair treatment. It was not aimed at substituting the opinion of the judiciary or of individual judges for that of the relevant authority.

3 The court's function was to see that lawful authority was not abused by unfair treatment.

4 The court was not to attempt the task that the law entrusted to the relevant authority.

The above case was shortly followed by others in which the suitability of judicial review was raised in the House of Lords.

O'Reilly and others v Mackman and others (1982)

Millbanks v Secretary of State for Home Department and others (1982)

Following a riot at Hull Prison several prisoners were charged with offences under the Prison Rules and after they were found guilty the prisoners were penalised. Subsequently the prisoners instituted civil actions on the basis that the Prison Rules had been breached and there had been a breach of natural justice in the proceedings.

The Law Lords held that it would be contrary to public policy and an abuse of the process of the court for a person alleging infringement of his rights by a public authority to proceed by way of ordinary action rather than by an application for judicial review and in that way evade the protection given to public authorities by the rules governing applications for judicial review.

However, exceptions to the general rule arising out of private law rights or where none of the parties objected were to be admitted and other exceptions decided on a case-by-case basis.

There are several forms of administrative action that may be judicially examined; in this handbook the following are outlined – an appropriate legal textbook should be consulted if further details are required:

- *Ultra vires* or illegal actions.
- Improper use of discretionary powers.
- Actions contrary to the rules of natural justice or unfair actions.
- Actions containing errors of law on the face of the record, sometimes said to be unreasonable or irrational actions.
- Decisions made that are contrary to the European Union principle of proportionality.

Ultra vires

By definition, a statutory body can only do those things that it is authorised to do; therefore any act or omission which is outside the compass of the statutory authority is outside the law. This is termed an *ultra vires* act, which means, literally, 'beyond the power'.

Following are some examples of *ultra vires* actions:

- Having no jurisdiction or authority to take action in the particular circumstances.
- Exceeding statutory powers by doing more than the law actually authorises.

- Making procedural errors whilst carrying out a legal action. This commonly occurs when a public body does not give notice to the correct people, in the proper form, of a proposed action.

The Commission for Racial Equality was criticised by the House of Lords in 1984 when it was held that it had no power to launch an investigation into racial discrimination by an organisation **unless** it believed unlawful acts had occurred. It was held that going on 'fishing expeditions' was clearly in excess of its powers under the Race Relations Act 1976 and the fact that it had subsequently found evidence of discrimination did not validate an originally illegal action.

Even those holding the highest offices in the land are not immune to a review of actions alleged to be in excess of their statutory powers. The first case related to the issue of warrants by the Home Secretary:

R v Secretary of State for Home Affairs ex parte Ruddock (1987)

In this case three leading members of the Campaign for Nuclear Disarmament sought a decision by judicial review that the actions of the Home Secretary in authorising telephone taps on CND members was illegal. There were two points decided in this case:

1 The aggrieved persons **had the right to seek judicial review** in cases alleging an abuse of power by government authorities although it was accepted as in *Malone v Metropolitan Commissioner* (1979) that English courts had no power to enforce the Human Rights Convention.

2 With regard to the legality of the warrant, the court held that it was issued outside the criteria, but this did not amount to ministerial misfeasance.

For further comments on telephone tapping see page 42 *et seq*.

In the next case the minister's actions were found to be illegal and in consequence they were quashed by the court.

R v Secretary of State for Social Services ex parte Cotton (1985)

The Secretary of State was not empowered by the Supplementary Benefits Act 1976 to make regulations enabling himself to fix the maximum amount and other details of supplementary benefit payable to young people. The regulations were *ultra vires* and a declaration to that effect was granted.

Improper use of discretionary powers

Many statutes give public bodies discretion in respect of the detailed performance of their duties. Consider, for example, the extent of the discretion of a chief constable. Following are some aspects of discretion that are subject to the control of the judiciary:

- Improperly delegating a discretionary power.

- Failing to exercise a discretion properly because of one of the following reasons:

- exercising discretionary power under the dictation or control of another person or body;
- fettering discretion by previously making rules that preclude using discretion in any individual case;
- by the body binding itself not to exercise discretion if that would disable itself from fulfilling its primary statutory purpose;
- failing to recognise the extent of the discretion that is authorised by the statute.

Abusing discretionary power is a more serious situation and may come about by the public body:

- exercising the discretion for an improper purpose not authorised by law;
- being influenced by irrelevant grounds or by ignoring relevant considerations and thus making a quite unreasonable decision;
- making unreasonable use of discretionary power to the detriment of the rights of private citizens; or
- exercising the discretionary power in bad faith; in other words, fraud or malice affects any decision.

An example of the improper delegation of a discretionary power was seen in the following case:

R v Derbyshire Police Authority ex parte Wilson and another (1989)

When considering whether to reimburse police officers and the Police Federation for the costs of legal expenses incurred by the officers, a police authority could not accept the recommendations of a panel appointed to hear submissions, since it had not delegated the decision to the panel, and therefore the authority had to consider the matter and make the decision itself. The decision refusing to pay legal expenses was quashed.

A case which involved the fettering of discretion was seen in:

R v Secretary of State for the Home Department ex parte Hastrup (1996)

It was held that a minister of the Crown would fetter his discretion unlawfully if he laid down a policy which had to be applied rigidly in particular cases.

The High Court will not interfere with decisions based on the lawful use of discretionary power and several judges have said that the court will not substitute its discretion for that of the public body but it will ensure that discretion is used lawfully and within the confines of the particular statute. In cases were the statutory power directs that the discretion can be exercised on, say, 'reasonable grounds'; 'with reasonable cause' or 'on reasonable suspicion'; the court can inquire to ensure that the conditions precedent have been met.

The application of discretionary powers by chief constables has been examined on several occasions, notably in *R v Metropolitan Police Commissioner ex parte Blackburn* (1968) and *R v Chief Constable of Sussex ex parte International Traders' Ferry Ltd* (1997), see details on pages 57 and 59. In these, and other cases the courts have examined particular actions in order to ascertain that the particular chief constable has used his discretion in a lawful and reasonable manner.

Natural justice

The principles of natural justice apply, not only to courts of law, but also to any administrative body acting judicially or quasi-judicially. The duty to act judicially exists where any body of persons has legal authority to determine questions affecting the rights of subjects.

In cases of dispute, the court will decide whether, or not, a particular act is a judicial one as a matter of fact.

Judicial actions are frequently discipline hearings in some form or other. When examining such cases the court will look to see that the individual has had a fair hearing and will ensure certain fundamental principles of justice have been followed:

- A man may not be a judge in his own cause (this means that, for example, a chief constable cannot try a discipline case when he is a witness).
- No party ought to be condemned unheard and he must know in good time the cause which he has to meet. (This is why an investigating officer must give the officer concerned details of the complaint made against him as soon as possible.)
- A party is entitled to know the reason for the decision reached.

An example of the first principle is:

R v Chief Constable of South Wales ex parte Thornhill (1987)

The presence of the deputy chief constable, who was effectively the prosecutor in disciplinary proceedings against the applicant, in the room of the chief constable who was at the time deliberating on his decision in those proceedings, did not, where it was explained that such presence was for a purpose unconcerned with those proceedings, amount to a breach of the rules of natural justice.

The leading case and other examples of the second principle that relate to police are:

Ridge v Baldwin (1964)

Brighton Watch Committee purported to dismiss chief constable Ridge after he was involved in criminal proceedings. The dismissal took place in Ridge's absence and he was given no opportunity to state his case.

The House of Lords declared that the decision was contrary to natural justice and the Watch Committee decision was quashed.

R v Chief Constable of Merseyside Police ex parte Calveley and others (1985)

The Court of Appeal quashed the disciplinary tribunal's decision because the officers were not informed officially of any complaints about their conduct until some two and a half years after the relevant incident had occurred and an investigator had been appointed.

This involved a breach of regulation 7 of the Police (Discipline) Regulations 1977 which provided that 'the investigating officer shall, as soon as practicable ... in writing inform the member subject to investigation of the ... complaint.' There had, in the judgment of the Court of Appeal, been so serious a departure from the disciplinary procedure that the court should in the exercise of its discretion grant judicial review and set aside the decision of the relevant tribunal, namely, the chief constable.

[This case later went to the House of Lords to consider other matters in respect of civil liability.]

R v Chief Constable of North Wales Police Force ex parte Connah (1986)

A police officer charged with a disciplinary offence should be allowed to interview, without a senior officer present, potential witnesses who were employees of the police force, if failure to do so meant he was being unfairly or unreasonably hindered in the preparation of his defence.

R v Chief Constable of Avon and Sommerset ex parte Clarke (1986)

Where force procedure required a chief constable, before dispensing with the services of a probationary officer, to reach his decision upon a file which included a record of the probationer's comments on what was said against him, it was not sufficient, in most cases for the chief constable to receive only a summarised and edited account of the probationer's case from the investigating officer who was also making an adverse recommendation against the probationer.

The chief constable's decision was quashed and the probationer was regarded as having been on unpaid leave from the date of the purported dismissal.

Errors of law

It can usually be taken that an error of law has occurred when, on a correct statement of the law, the public body could not have reached the decision that it did. A wrong decision is not itself grounds for review as it must be shown that:

- the decision was reached for the wrong reasons; or
- the record must show that relevant evidence was ignored; or
- the public body refused to hear the evidence.

Note that a public body given discretion to reach a decision may believe or refuse to accept facts that are put in evidence. This discretion will not be questioned by the courts providing the matter was dealt with in a manner conforming to all of the legal rules governing the subject.

R v Director of Government Communications Headquarters ex parte Hedges (1988)

A decision to withdraw a person's positive vetting was made in the interests of national security and, therefore, the question whether it was reasonable was not amenable to review by the court. Accordingly, the court could not decide whether a decision to remove the applicant's positive vetting, made on the grounds that there was doubt about his discretion and reliability because of his homosexual relationships, was unreasonable. However, the court could consider whether the decision had been reached fairly.

European Union principle of proportionality

This is an important general principle recognised in European Union law which is applied to constrain public authorities from imposing obligations beyond those needed to achieve the objective of the measure concerned.

The principle says, in effect, that the means needed to reach the ends of the legislation must be reasonable and that the advantage to the public must be greater than the disadvantage.

In *R v Chief Constable of Sussex ex parte International Trader's Ferry Ltd* (1995) at the first hearing before the QBD Court, it was held that the Chief Constable's action in restricting safe passage to the vehicles carrying exports came within this principle. This was on the basis that a decision regarding public order considerations had also affected UK treaty obligations in that it had caused an unlawful restriction on the level of exports. When the case went to the Court of Appeal this argument was rejected, see page 59 for further details of this case.

Remedies provided by the High Court

Following judicial review, if the public body has acted unlawfully, the High Court can order a number of remedies, and will use whatever is appropriate in the light of the original writ and the nature of the complaint.

- Awarding the aggrieved person damages.
- Giving a declaration that the order, act or decision of the public body is quashed. This means it is annulled or set aside. It is then open to the public body, if it wishes and if it can do so, to re-process the action or decision in a lawful way.
- Reversing or varying an order or decision on the basis that it was reached with an error of law.
- Making an authoritative statement of the law governing a particular legal dispute which will then be binding on inferior courts.
- Making a declaration that a particular administrative act or order (eg by-laws) are *ultra vires* and therefore of no legal standing.
- Restraining the performance or continuance of an unlawful action by:
  - an order of prohibition (a court order banning any action that is in excess of power or an abuse of power);
  - an injunction (a court order banning the carrying on or starting of a particular act);
  - a declaration (a formal statement by the court stating the rights of the parties).
- Making an order to secure the performance of a public duty by:
  - an order of *mandamus* (a court order commanding a person or body to perform a public duty);
  - a declaration (a formal statement by the court stating the rights of the parties);

    ○ a mandatory injunction (a court order commanding that a particular act be carried out).
- Making an order of *certiorari* directing an inferior tribunal to send a record of the proceedings in issue to the High Court for consideration and, if appropriate, quashing.

In some cases the High Court has shown the extent of its powers in particular circumstances.

Re M, House of Lords (1993)

The court has jurisdiction in judicial review proceedings to grant interim and final injunctions against an officer of the Crown and to make a finding of contempt against a government department or a minister of the Crown in his official capacity.

In July 1996 the Inland Revenue came under the scrutiny of the High Court for an alleged contempt in the following case:

R v Commissioners of Inland Revenue and others ex parte Kingston Smith (1996)

It was held that it was not open to officers of the Inland Revenue to disregard the terms of an injunction obtained by telephone from the duty judge at the Royal Courts of Justice, nor was it possible for those officers to seek to negotiate away the effect of that injunction with the applicants.

The judge said that the court had found itself in the unwelcome position of having to pursue serious breaches of one of its orders. It was to be understood that in so doing it was acting under its duty to uphold the rule of law. The court's remedies could include committal and sequestration.

A similar case occurred in February 1997 when the Director of the Serious Fraud Office and four senior officers were taken to court for contempt in failing to obey a High Court injunction during the course of an investigation.

R v City of London Magistrates' Court and another ex parte Green (1997)

The injunction prohibited the 'downloading' of computer-held information until a full court hearing could take place. However, SFO officers continued to download information for about six hours after the injunction was issued.

The word 'download' was at issue with the SFO claiming it meant transferring information from a computer to a storage device and then writing the image to a compact disc. The court held that the mere transfer of data from one storage device to another was the appropriate definition.

The contempt action was dismissed and it was said that although there was an obligation strictly to comply with the terms of an injunction, the courts would only punish a person for contempt upon adequate proof that:

(1) the terms of the injunction were clear and unambiguous;

(2) the particular defendant in the contempt proceedings had proper notice of such terms; and

(3) he had broken those terms.

In the present case neither (1) nor (2) had been met.

Every public official should be fully aware of the powers that the High Court possesses when supervising improper actions breaching the rights of ordinary citizens.

13   Police Complaints Authority

Part IV Police Act 1996 consolidates and clarifies Part IX Police and Criminal Evidence Act 1984. However, this part of the 1996 Act did not commence at the same time as the remainder of it. New disciplinary regulations for the police are being discussed and are anticipated in 1998 when it is assumed Part IV will commence. All references in this chapter relate to the 1996 Police Act.

Overview of Part IV Police Act 1996

Following is an outline of the matters covered by the sections in Part IV Police Act 1996.

Part IV Complaints, disciplinary proceedings, etc

Chapter I – Complaints

Section 65 Interpretation of phrases used in Chapter I.

Section 66 Authorises the existence of the Police Complaints Authority (PCA).

Section 67 Describes the procedures to be followed in the preliminary handling of complaints against members of a police force.

Section 68 Describes the procedures to be followed by police authorities when complaints are received about chief or assistant chief constables.

Section 69 The standard investigation procedure to be followed by a chief constable following receipt of a complaint about a member of his force who is not an assistant chief constable.

Section 70 The circumstances under which a complaint should be referred to the PCA.

Section 71 The referring of other matters to the PCA.

Section 72 The supervision of investigations into complaints and other matters by the PCA.

Section 73 To whom reports are sent at the conclusion of an investigation supervised by the PCA.

Section 74 The steps to be taken after investigation into the conduct of a chief or assistant chief constable.

Section 75 The steps to be taken after investigation into the conduct of another member of the police force.

Section 76 The powers of the PCA to recommend and direct a chief constable to institute disciplinary proceedings against a member of his force when he has not done so.

Section 77 Police authorities and HM inspectors of constabulary are to keep themselves informed as to the manner of dealing with complaints in police forces.

Section 78 Extends relations of the PCA to other authorities, eg British Transport Police, etc.

Section 79 Statutory reports to be made by the PCA.

Section 80 Restriction on the disclosure of information by members or servants of the PCA.

Section 81 Authority for the Home Secretary to make regulations concerning the procedures to be followed in this chapter.

Section 82 Procedures for making regulations under section 81.

Section 83 Authority for the Home Secretary to issue guidance to police authorities, chief constable and other members of police forces concerning the discharge of their duties when dealing with complaints.

Chapter II – Disciplinary and other proceedings

Section 84 Legal representation at disciplinary and other proceedings.

Section 85 Form of appeal in cases involving dismissal, requirement to resign or reduction in rank.

Section 86 No statement made for the purpose of informal resolution of a complaint is admissible in subsequent criminal, civil or disciplinary proceedings.

Section 87 Authority for the Home Secretary to issue guidance to police authorities, chief constable and other members of police forces concerning the discharge of their duties when dealing with disciplinary matters.

Section 88 The chief constable has vicarious liability for torts committed by members of his police force.
[This section is in force, see Chapter 15 for further details.]

The establishment of the Police Complaints Authority

From the 1960s onward there was a lot of public disquiet regarding the way in which complaints concerning the conduct of police officers was dealt with. It was commonly said in the press that police investigated 'their own', acted as judge and jury then whitewashed the improper behaviour.

Pressures mounted for an independent body to oversee complaints against the police, the police disputed the need for such a body, broadly on two grounds:

- only serving police officers possessed the necessary investigative skills to examine complaints; and
- such a body would make police officers vulnerable to false and malicious complaints designed to deter them from carrying out their duties properly.

The Police Complaints Board (PCB) was instituted by the Police Act 1976 but it was ill-conceived and was heavily criticised by both police and public.

Following the criticism, in 1984 the PCB was transmuted into the Police Complaints Authority (PCA) with new powers defined in the Police and Criminal Evidence Act 1984. The PCA is an independent body corporate (section 66) and its constitution and membership provisions are detailed in Schedule 5 Police Act 1996. Although it is, in legal terms, an independent body it should not be overlooked that investigations are carried out by serving police officers under its supervision and not by independent investigators.

Duties of the Police Complaints Authority

The PCA deals with the most serious complaints about police conduct and matters that are likely to be of public concern, it is easier to overview its supervisory task by means of a diagram.

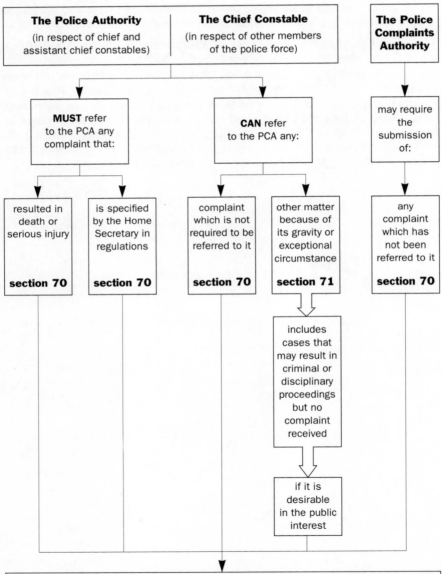

After receipt of the report from the investigating officer the PCA will (section 73):

- submit a statement to the police authority or chief constable as appropriate;
- if practicable, send a copy to the member of the force whose conduct was investigated;
- if the investigation related to a complaint from a member of the public and it is practicable to do so will send a copy to the complainant.

Sections 74 and 75 detail the steps to be taken that will lead to either criminal or discipline proceedings if they are appropriate. This includes the responsibility placed upon the chief constable to report to his police authority giving details of the case, including reasons for not taking discipline proceedings.

The PCA has been prepared to use judicial review procedures in cases where it has deemed the actions of chief constables to be inappropriate, such as:

R v Metropolitan Police Disciplinary Tribunal ex parte Police Complaints Authority (1992)

If false statements had been made by police officers at the trial of a convicted defendant, those statements could form the subject of disciplinary proceedings against the officers even though the conviction stood. The court quashed a decision by the Metropolitan Police Disciplinary Tribunal that disciplinary proceedings should not go ahead in this particular case.

In the following case the PCA challenged a decision to dismiss disciplinary charges and permit the police officer to retire from the force on pension.

R v Chief Constable of Devon and Cornwall ex parte Police Complaints Authority (1996)

A chief constable was invited by the investigating officer in a disciplinary proceeding to require the defending officer to retire from the force. He dismissed the proceedings and accepted the officer's retirement.

The court held that a chief constable has to weigh the interests of both the police service and the public in seeing that disciplinary proceedings go through to their end. Chief constables must make a clear separation of their prosecutorial and judicial functions from their overall administration of their police force. An order of *certiorari* was made quashing the decision to dismiss disciplinary charges and ordering that they should be heard on their substantive merit.

[In subsequent discipline proceedings the defending officer was cleared of a charge of neglect of duty.]

Police Appeals Tribunal

A member of a police force who is dismissed, required to resign or reduced in rank following discipline procedures has the right to appeal against the decision to the Police Appeals Tribunal (section 85 and sections 38 and 82 PA 1997).

The Tribunal is authorised to require by summons any person to attend a hearing to give evidence or to produce documents. Evidence may be taken on oath from witnesses. Anyone who refuses or deliberately fails to attend or who falsifies documents he has been required to produce commits an offence (section 85 and section 250 Local Government Act 1972).

After the appeal hearing the Tribunal can, in appropriate cases, reduce the severity of the penalty.

The chairman of the Tribunal must be a legally qualified person and details of its composition and procedures are contained in Schedule 6.

Other discipline matters

Less serious complaints and discipline matters are resolved without the intervention of the PCA, they are dealt with internally in each force.

Strict rules are laid down and most of Part IV of the Act consists of detailed descriptions of the procedures to be followed on the receipt of a complaint against a police officer, the subsequent investigation and the criminal or discipline procedures that can ensue. The Act is amplified by disciplinary regulations that define specific breaches of discipline. The discipline offences are grouped under the following headings:

- discreditable conduct;
- misconduct towards another member of the police force;
- disobedience to orders;
- neglect of duty;
- falsehood and prevarication;
- improper disclosure of information;
- corrupt or improper practice;
- abuse of authority;
- racially discriminatory behaviour;
- neglect of health;
- improper dress or untidiness;
- damage to police property;
- drunkenness;
- drinking alcohol on duty or soliciting alcoholic drink;
- entering licensed premises other than for an authorised purpose;
- criminal conduct; and
- being an accessory to a disciplinary offence.

It is not, perhaps, surprising that in an area of such complicated procedures the courts have been called upon to resolve some points of contention. Some of the issues raised in these cases will be found in the section titled 'Natural justice', page 107 *et seq* and under 'Civil law – disciplinary matters', page 161.

14 Supervision of Covert Policing

The Security Service

Before the Security Service Act 1989 the only formal procedure to follow by a person aggrieved at something done by the Security Service was to seek redress through the courts.

In 1987 three members of CND complained about the surveillance carried out on them by the Security Service. They sought judicial review, see *R v Secretary of State for Home Affairs ex parte Ruddock* (1987), page 105. At the hearing it was confirmed that there was a right to judicial review of the actions of Security Service in these circumstances.

At about the same time two women named Harmon and Hewitt of the National Council for Civil Liberties took their case for invasion of privacy to the European Court of Human Rights, see page 37. Whilst this case was in progress the government of the day introduced legislation to regularise the legal position of the Security Service. The same legislation provided an institutional framework for dealing with complaints about actions of officers of the Security Service.

As new procedures had been introduced the European Commission did not award the women any compensation, leaving such questions to be dealt with in Britain.

The two women applied to the new Security Service Tribunal for files maintained on them to be destroyed. The tribunal decided that it had no power to act on any files opened before the commencement of the 1989 Act and therefore took no action.

Harmon and Hewitt then sought a judicial review of the tribunal's decision which seemed to be contrary to at least the 'spirit' of the European judgment. However, the High Court ruled that it had no power to make any such declaration as the 1989 Act clearly states that tribunal decisions cannot be questioned in a court. Additionally, the judge pointed out that the applications had not been made promptly enough.

The Security Service Commissioner

The Prime Minister must appoint a person who holds or has held high judicial office as the Security Service Commissioner (section 4 SS Act). The Commissioner is responsible for:

- investigating complaints about the Service;
- reviewing the exercise of the Home Secretary's powers in issuing warrants;
- making an annual report on the discharge of his functions to the Prime Minister;

- when necessary reporting to the Prime Minister on any other matter concerning his functions.

It is the statutory duty of:

- every member of the Security Service; and
- every official of the Home Department

to disclose to the Commissioner any documents or information that he may require (section 4 SS Act).

The Prime Minister must lay before Parliament a copy of the annual report made by the Commissioner together with a statement as to whether any matter has been excluded from that copy on the grounds that it would be prejudicial to security (section 4 SS Act).

The Security Service Tribunal

A tribunal for the purpose of investigating complaints about the Security Service has been instituted (section 5 and Schedule 1 SS Act). Its membership and procedures are defined in Schedule 2 SS Act

The Commissioner is directed to give the Tribunal all such assistance in discharging their functions as they may require (section 5 SS Act).

Actions following the investigation of a complaint

When, following the investigation of a complaint, the Tribunal or the Commissioner has reached a decision, they will:

- give notice to the complainant that the findings are, or are not, in his favour; and
- make a report of their findings to the Home Secretary and the Commissioner.

Remedial action that can be taken in proven cases may be:

- the destruction of any records containing improperly acquired or incorrect information;
- the payment of suitable compensation to the aggrieved person;
- the quashing of any warrant that has been improperly issued.

Immunity from review

The decisions of the tribunal and the Commissioner shall not be subject to appeal or liable to be questioned in any court (section 5 SS Act) as seen in the *Harmon and Hewitt* case mentioned above.

Other similar bodies

There are similar statutory arrangements for a Commissioner, Tribunal and the receiving of complaints under:

- the Interception of Communications Act 1985; and
- the Intelligence Services Act 1994.

Both Acts contain the *caveat* that decisions of the Commissioner or Tribunal can not be reviewed in the courts.

Supervision of police covert operations

Special Branch

Members of a police force employed on special branch duties have the same authority and accountability as any other constable. They are answerable to the same judicial control, complaints procedures, civil and criminal laws as other constables. See guidelines on pages 41–42.

Commissioners supervising police surveillance operations

The Prime Minister has power to appoint a Chief Commissioner and other Commissioners to oversee police operations involving the interference or damage to property or telecommunications, that is, installing surveillance equipment (section 91 PA 1997).

All of the Commissioners must be persons who hold or have held high judicial office. The appointments last for three years but they may be renewed.

Any person having functions under the Act, or acting in relation to an authorisation must comply with any request by a Commissioner to produce documents or information required by the Commissioner in the discharge of his functions (section 107 PA 1997).

The decisions of the Chief Commissioner or any other Commissioner in these matters is not subject to appeal or liable to be questioned in any court of law (section 91 PA 1997).

Authorisation for entry, etc

A police Authorising Officer must get the approval of a Commissioner in certain specified circumstances (section 97 PA 1997). Details of these procedures are on pages 44–45.

Complaints about police actions

An aggrieved person may make a complaint to a Commissioner about police surveillance activities (section 102 PA 1997). The Commissioner will inquire into the matter and if the complaint is upheld that police actions do not conform to the statute, he can (section 103 PA 1997):

- quash the authorisation;
- order the destruction of any records relating to the information obtained as a result of the quashed authorisation. This would not include any records that are required for pending criminal or civil proceedings.

After taking such action the commissioner must report in writing to the Authorising Officer and the Chief Commissioner giving his findings (section 103 PA 1997).

Appeals against a Commissioner's decision

If either the complainant or the Authorising Officer is dissatisfied by the Commissioner's decision, an appeal against that decision can be made to the Chief Commissioner (sections 104 and 106 PA 1997). The Chief Commissioner's decision is final and binding.

After determining the appeal the Chief Commissioner must give notice of his decision to (section 105 PA 1997):

- the Authorising Officer concerned;
- the Commissioner concerned;
- the complainant; and

in any case in which he dismisses the appeal, to:

- the Prime Minister.

The detailed procedures relating to the operation of the foregoing matters are laid down in Part III and Schedule 7 Police Act 1997.

The Chief Commissioner

It is the duty of the Chief Commissioner to keep under review the performance of functions under the Act. He must make an annual report to the Prime Minister regarding his duties and, additionally, may report to him at any time on any matter that concerns him (section 105 PA 1997).

The Prime Minister must lay a copy of the annual report before Parliament but may exclude any matter that would be prejudicial to the prevention or detection of serious crime.

Part V

The application of civil law to members of police forces

15 Civil Liability, Remedies and Public Interest Immunity

Overview

Civil law, in contrast to criminal and administrative law, regulates the conduct of persons in their direct relations with each other. The 1929 Royal Commission on the Police made it quite clear that police officers are answerable to the courts in the same way as any other citizen; thus if a constable infringes the rights of another citizen he will be accountable to the courts.

Civil liability

When the law gives someone a *right*, it automatically imposes on all others the duty of observing that right. Anyone who disregards the right may be *sued* in the civil courts by the aggrieved person to seek a *remedy*. The person bringing the action is called the *plaintiff*. The civil courts will seek to put a plaintiff who proves his case into the same position as he was before the wrong was committed.

When a person commits an act or omission that breaches the law, he is said to have *legal liability*; this means that he is answerable to a court of law. There are several different forms of liability, the following are significant in the context of this part of the handbook.

Absolute liability

Certain laws place responsibility on particular persons for breaches of the law, irrespective of whether the breach was committed deliberately, recklessly or negligently. Strict liability is not exactly the same as absolute liability, but for the purpose of the handbook the two can be considered the same.

Some criminal laws relating to licensing and drugs abuse place an absolute liability on such people as licensees and the owners of property. In civil law an example of absolute liability is the duty placed on employers to ensure the safety of employees at their place of work.

Vicarious liability

It is a *presumption of law* that an employer is responsible for the acts done in the course of an employee's work as it is assumed that such acts are performed with the express or implied authority of the employer.

EMPLOYER **EMPLOYEE** **THIRD PARTY**

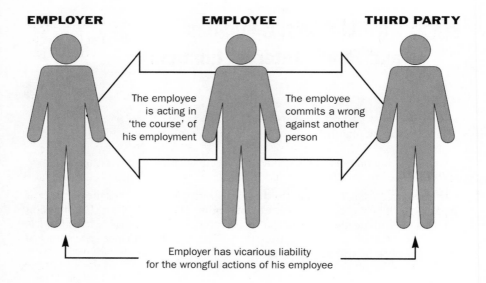

The employee is acting in 'the course' of his employment

The employee commits a wrong against another person

Employer has vicarious liability
for the wrongful actions of his employee

It follows this assumption that if damage is caused to another person by his employee during the course of employment, the employer as well as the employee will be liable. This is called the *vicarious liability* of the employer.

It was decided in *Fisher v Oldham Corporation* (1930) (see page 25), that a constable is not a servant of either the police authority or the chief constable.

In past years this meant that any injured plaintiff could only take action against the constable himself as neither the police authority nor the chief constable could be held to have vicarious liability for any wrongful action committed by a constable on duty.

This had two effects on any potential litigation:

- it was unlikely that a constable would be able to pay for his defence in an action for tort. Although, from 1931, police authorities usually gave support, providing the action complained of was done in good faith in the intended execution of his duty; and
- it was equally unlikely that a successful litigant would receive any compensation awarded to him as the constable would be described in legal terms as a man of straw, ie having no financial substance.

The 1962 Royal Commission on the Police raised this matter and recommended that the situation should be changed and this was done in the Police Act 1964. The matter is now covered in section 88 which states:

> The chief officer of police ... shall be liable in respect of torts committed by constables under his direction and control in the performance or purported performance of their functions in like manner as a master is liable in respect of torts committed by his servants in the course of their employment, and accordingly shall ... be treated ... as a joint tortfeasor. [See page 139 for the definition of tort.] Any damages or costs awarded against the chief officer will be paid from the police fund.

In the case of constables working in the NCIS or NCS, the vicarious liability is attached to the respective Directors General (sections 42 and 86 PA 1997). For officers seconded to other common service duties, the Home Secretary has vicarious liability.

It must be emphasised that for vicarious liability to exist the constable must be acting in the course of his employment as was shown in the following case:

Makanjuola v Commissioner of Police of the Metropolis and another (1989)

In this case the plaintiff was in the country on the basis of a visitor's permit and had applied for a student's permit that she had not at the time received. She had taken part-time work which was in contravention of the visitor's permit but which would have been legitimate under a student's permit. She was visited by a police constable who questioned her and claimed that there were irregularities that could lead to her deportation. He offered to refrain from reporting in return for sexual favours and in consequence she submitted to sexual assaults including buggery.

Following other matters the plaintiff reported these assaults several months later and subsequently she instigated civil action for trespass to the person, assault and battery and intimidation by the constable. She also claimed that the Commissioner was vicariously liable for the actions of the constable.

The court found the constable liable and he was ordered to pay damages. However, it was held that the Commissioner was not vicariously liable for the torts that the constable had committed under threat for a purpose that was clearly a venture of his own.

Vicarious liability – legal points

For an employer to be vicariously liable three elements must be proved:

1 There must be an employment relationship between the worker who committed the tort and the defendant employer.
2 The employee must have committed a tort.
3 The tort must have been committed during the course of the employee's employment.

The first element is covered by section 88 and element two is a question of fact that has to be decided in each individual case. However, the third element causes a lot of legal dispute as it is not always easy to say whether particular actions were implemented during the course of the individual's employment.

In criminal law disputes often arise in cases of assaulting or obstructing a constable in the execution of his duty (section 89) (see page 11 *et seq*). The disputes centre on questions of fact whether the constable was, or was not, acting in the execution of his duty at the time of the incident. Similarly, there is a considerable body of case law regarding the basic point whether the employee committed the tort 'during the course of his employment' or not.

Each claim of vicarious liability has to be examined on its own facts although the general rule accepted by the courts is that an employee is within the course of his employment if, at the time of the tortious act, he was undertaking some authorised activity. The courts have tended to look at vicarious liability cases under two headings, *intentional wrongs* and *negligent acts*.

Vicarious liability – intentional wrongs by the employee

The following cases are a few examples of intentional wrongs. Most of them are not police cases, but parallels can be drawn with activities that could occur in a police setting. The decisions are highlighted by the author.

Heasmans v Clarity Cleaning Ltd (1987)

In this case the employee's job was to clean the plaintiff's offices and whilst so doing he used their telephone to make international calls costing £1,411. Held by the Court of Appeal that he was employed to clean the telephones, not to use them, he was therefore doing an unauthorised act outside the scope of his employment. **The employer was not vicariously liable.**

Irving v Post Office (1987)

A Post Office worker was authorised to write on letters to ensure their correct delivery. He wrote offensive remarks ('Go back to Jamaica Sambo') on a letter addressed to one of his neighbours with whom he was not on speaking terms. The Court of Appeal held that his wrongful act could not be regarded as being merely an unauthorised way of performing an authorised act but was wholly outside the sphere of his employment. **The Post Office was not vicariously liable for his act.**

Racz v Home Office (1993)

The plaintiff, a remand prisoner, refused to perform cleaning duties and was moved to a strip cell. Subsequently he claimed damages for assault, negligence and misfeasance by holders of public office, he also claimed that the Home Office was vicariously liable for the officers who, motivated by malice, moved him to the strip cell knowing they had no power under the Prison Rules to do so. The House of Lords held that the **Home Office could be vicariously liable for the acts of prison officers amounting to misfeasance in a public office unless it could be shown that their acts were so unconnected with their authorised duties as to be independent of and outside them.** This was a question of fact to be decided at the trial.

Farah v Commissioner of Police of the Metropolis (1996)

Police officers were subject to the Race Relations Act 1976 so that it was unlawful for them to discriminate in the provision of services, including the provision of protection from crime. But while a claim might be maintained against individual officers, **the chief officer of police was not vicariously liable** for their acts of racial discrimination.

[See page 25 for further details of this case.]

W v Commissioner of Police of the Metropolis (1997)

A woman constable complained of sexual assault by a fellow constable in a police section house. She alleged that she suffered mental illness as a consequence of the way she was treated by senior officers following her complaint. It was held that as this matter did not relate to operational circumstances, **the Commissioner could not be vicariously liable.**

[See page 158 for further details of case.]

When an employer has forbidden the employee to do certain things, and the employee, disregarding the instruction, nonetheless does the forbidden thing, the employer may still be liable if the instruction relates to the way in which the duty is to be performed. The employer might escape liability if the specific act itself is forbidden.

Limpus v London General Omnibus Co (1862)

The plaintiff's bus was overturned when the driver of the defendant's bus drove across it so as to be the first at a bus stop. The defendant's driver admitted that the act was intentional and arose out of bad feeling between the two drivers. The defendants had issued strict instructions to their drivers that they were not to obstruct other omnibuses. **Vicarious liability was held to exist** as the driver was acting within the scope of his employment at the time of the collision and it did not matter that the employer had expressly forbidden him to act as he did.

Rand (Joseph) Ltv v Craig (1919)

The employees were taking rubbish from a site and depositing it on the employer's dump. They were working on a bonus scheme related to the number of loads per day which they dumped. Employees were strictly forbidden from tipping rubbish other than on the authorised dump but some of the employees deposited their loads on another person's property which was nearer. The **employer was not vicariously liable** for damages as the employees were employed to take the rubbish from one definite place to another definite place.

If the employee commits a criminal act during the course of his employment, the employer may be liable for damages, depending upon the facts of the particular case:

Lloyd v Grace, Smith & Co (1912)

Smith was a solicitor who employed Sandies as a managing clerk. Mrs Lloyd owned two properties and had lent money on a mortgage but was not satisfied with the income. She sought advice from Sandies who advised her to sell the properties, call in the mortgage and re-invest the proceeds. Mrs Lloyd signed two deeds at Sandies' request which, unknown to her, transferred the properties and the mortgage to him. The **firm of solicitors was held to be vicariously liable** even though the fraud was entirely for the employee's benefit.

Morris v CW Martin & Sons Ltd (1966)

A mink stole was sent to a furrier for cleaning and whilst with the cleaners the fur was stolen by an employee. The employer had no reason to suppose that the employee was dishonest but as the thief had been entrusted with the fur during the course of his employment the **employer had vicarious liability** for the criminal act.

Vicarious liability – negligent actions by the employee

In some cases of negligent acts the courts have been willing to find that an employee has acted within the course of his employment. Following are examples:

Century Insurance Co v Northern Ireland Road Transport Board (1942)

The driver of a petrol tanker was transferring petrol to an underground tank when he lit a cigarette and threw the match to the floor. The resultant fire and explosion caused considerable damage. It was held that the **employer was liable** for the driver's actions as he discharged his duties under his contract of service in a negligent manner.

Smith v Stages (1989)

The plaintiff suffered serious injury in a car accident caused by the negligence of a fellow employee. The two employees had been sent from Stafford to Pembroke on an urgent job. They worked all day Sunday and Sunday night and were paid wages for eight hours sleeping time and eight hours travelling time; they were not required to be back at work in Stafford until Wednesday morning. The two men decided to return home immediately after completing the Sunday night shift and on the journey home were involved in the accident. The House of Lords held that, as the employee who was driving was being paid wages for the journey home, he was acting in the course of his employment. The decision to return was not a wise one, but though the men had been paid for sleeping time, they were not *required* to sleep, they had discretion about sleeping and the time of return. **The employer was held to be vicariously liable**.

Note that if Smith had been expressly directed to take a period of rest before returning the employer might have evaded vicarious liability as his action might have been outside the course of his duty.

In some cases of negligent actions, as with intentional actions, even though the employer expressly forbids a particular action, this might not exonerate him from liability.

Rose v Plenty (1976)

The employer expressly prohibited employees from allowing boys to ride on their milk floats. In spite of the ban an employee allowed a boy of 13 to ride on the milk float when helping him with his deliveries. The boy was injured whilst on the float due to the negligence of the employee. The Court of Appeal held that the employee driver was acting within the course of his employment at the time of the accident. **The employer had vicarious liability**.

Damages awarded against an employer

If damages are awarded against an employer as described above, he is entitled to sue the employee to recover the money paid, but this is not usually done as employers will normally have insurance cover against such eventualities.

Lancashire County Council v Municipal Mutual Insurance Ltd (1996)

It was not contrary to public policy for local authorities and chief constables to insure against their vicarious liability to pay damages, including exemplary damages, for the criminal acts of employees or, police officers.

Civil law remedies

The usual remedies provided by the courts for successful litigants are as follows.

Injunctions

- An injunction is a court order to stop doing the thing complained of, or, not to undertake a particular action in the future.
- A mandatory injunction is an order to carry out a particular task.

If the injunction is disobeyed the person concerned is considered to be in *contempt of court* and will be dealt with accordingly. This could involve either imprisonment or a financial penalty in some circumstances.

Pecuniary damages

Most civil actions are instigated in order to make the wrongdoer pay for the harm that has been caused. Damages (financial compensation) are awarded by a court to a successful plaintiff, they may be categorised in several different ways.

Compensatory damages

These damages are paid to compensate the plaintiff for the harm or injury that has been suffered. In cases were the injury is followed by a financial loss, the damages are called *special damages* which will be calculated in a way that places the plaintiff in the same position as he would have been had the wrong not been committed. This tends to be a fairly straightforward arithmetical calculation. In the end the plaintiff should neither suffer loss nor make a profit.

In cases were the harm includes unquantifiable things such as injury, loss of the use of some amenity, etc the damages for 'pain and suffering' are awarded broadly in accordance with a tariff scale authorised by the High Court. In cases were the plaintiff was partly at fault, the damages when calculated will be apportioned according to the degree of blame. Thus if a plaintiff was awarded £1,000 in damages, but was held to be 25% responsible for the accident, then he would receive £750.

Aggravated damages

If the court decides that the defendant's behaviour was such that the plaintiff suffered more than would be expected in such a case, disapproval of the defendant can be shown by awarding a greater or aggravated sum in damages in addition to the amount of *compensatory damages* awarded.

Punitive or exemplary damages

Punitive damages are awarded following behaviour by the defendant that is worse than that encountered in aggravated damages. The purpose is to punish the defendant and to deter others from similar behaviour in the future by awarding additional sums in addition to the *compensatory damages*. There are several classes of cases that attract punitive damages, including racial discrimination and other cases where such awards are permitted by statute. Additionally, when official bodies or individual officials behave in an arbitrary, oppressive or unconstitutional way punitive damages may be awarded.

Other categories of damages are *nominal damages* paid to a successful plaintiff who has suffered no loss when a small sum is awarded to show that his case was successful. *Contemptuous damages* are awarded (usually in libel actions) when the plaintiff has proved his case according to law but the court is of the opinion that the action should never have been taken to court; the award usually consists of the lowest legal tender coin.

The number of civil actions against the police has increased dramatically since the mid-1970s. This has probably been more a reflection of the extension of vicarious liability to the chief constable (section 88) than a significant change in police behaviour. By 1996 damages, sometimes in excess of £200,000 were being awarded by juries in cases of police misconduct and in February 1997 the Metropolitan Commissioner went to the Court of Appeal to seek judicial guidance on the level of these awards. The Lords of Appeal found as follows.

Thompson v Commissioner of Police of the Metropolis (1997)

The Court of Appeal defined guidelines as to the directions to be given to a jury assessing damages in civil actions against the police in order to establish some relationship between such awards and damages for personal injuries.

Guidance that should be given

While there was no formula which was appropriate for all cases and the precise form of a summing-up was very much a matter within the discretion of the trial judge, it was suggested that in many cases it would be convenient to include in a summing-up on the issue of damages additional directions on the following lines:

1 It should be explained to the jury that if they found in the plaintiff's favour the only remedy which they had power to grant was an award of damages. Save in exceptional situations such damages were only awarded as compensation and were intended to compensate the plaintiff for any injury or damage which he had suffered. They were not intended to punish the defendant.

2 As the law stood at present compensatory damages were of two types:

   (a) ordinary damages which the court would suggest should be described as basic; and

   (b) aggravated damages.

   Aggravated damages could only be awarded where they were claimed by the plaintiff and where there were aggravating features about the defendant's conduct which justified the award of aggravated damages.

   Where special damages were claimed in respect of some specific pecuniary loss that claim should be explained separately.

3 The jury should be told that the basic damages would depend on the circumstances and the degree of harm suffered by the plaintiff. But they should be provided with an appropriate bracket to use as a starting point. The judge would be responsible for determining the bracket, and the court envisaged that in the ordinary way the judge would have heard submissions on the matter from counsel in the absence of the jury.

4 In a straightforward case of wrongful arrest and imprisonment or malicious prosecution the jury should be informed of the approximate figure to be taken as the correct starting point for basic damages for the actual loss of liberty or for the wrongful prosecution, and also given an approximate ceiling figure. It should be explained that those were no more than guideline figures based on the judge's experience and on awards in other cases and the actual figure was one on which they must decide.

5 In a straightforward case of wrongful arrest and imprisonment the starting point was likely to be about £500 for the first hour during which the plaintiff had been deprived of his or her liberty. After the first hour an additional sum was to be awarded, but that sum should be on a reducing scale so as to keep the damages proportionate with those payable in personal injury cases and because the plaintiff was entitled to have a higher rate of compensation for the initial shock of being arrested. As a guideline the court considered, for example, that a plaintiff who had been wrongly kept in custody for 24 hours should for that alone normally be regarded as entitled to an award of about £3,000.

6 In the case of malicious prosecution, the figure should start at about £2,000 and for prosecution continuing for as long as two years, the case being taken to the crown court, an award of about £10,000 could be appropriate. If a malicious prosecution resulted in a conviction which was only set aside on an appeal that would justify a larger award to reflect the longer period during which the plaintiff had been in peril and had been caused distress.

7 The figures which the court had identified so far were provided to assist the judge in determining the bracket within which the jury should be invited to place their award. The court appreciated, however, that circumstances could vary dramatically from case to case and that those and subsequent figures which the court provided were not intended to be applied in a mechanistic manner.

8 If the case was one in which aggravated damages were claimed and could be appropriately awarded, the nature of aggravated damages should be explained to the jury.

Such damages could be awarded where there were aggravating features about the case which would result in the plaintiff not receiving sufficient compensation for the injury suffered if the award were restricted to a basic award.

Aggravating features could include humiliating circumstances at the time of the arrest or any conduct of those responsible for the arrest or the prosecution which showed that they had behaved in a highhanded, insulting, malicious or oppressive manner either in relation to the arrest or imprisonment or in conducting the prosecution.

Aggravating features could also include the way the litigation and trial were conducted.

9 The jury should then be told that if they considered the case was one for the award of damages other than basic damages then they should usually make a separate award for each category. That was contrary to the present practice but would result in greater transparency as to the make-up of the award.

10 Where it was appropriate to award aggravated damages the figure was unlikely to be less than £1,000. It was not possible to indicate a precise arithmetical relationship between basic damages and aggravated damages because the circumstances would vary from case to case. In the ordinary way, however, the court would not expect the aggravated damages to be as much as twice the basic damages except perhaps where, on the particular facts, the basic damages were modest.

11 It should be strongly emphasised to the jury that the total figure for basic and aggravated damages should not exceed what they considered was fair compensation for the injury which the plaintiff had suffered It should also be explained that if aggravated damages were awarded, such damages, although compensatory and not intended as a punishment, would in fact contain a penal element as far as the defendant was concerned.

12 Finally, the jury should be told in a case where exemplary damages were claimed and the judge considered that there was evidence to support such a claim, that although it was not normally possible to award damages with the object of punishing the defendant, exceptionally that was possible where there had been conduct, including oppressive or arbitrary behaviour, by police officers which deserved the exceptional remedy of exemplary damages. It should be explained to the jury:

(a) That if the jury were awarding aggravated damages those damages would have already provided compensation for the injury suffered by the plaintiff as a result of the oppressive and insulting behaviour of the police officer and, inevitably, a measure of punishment from the defendant's point of view.

(b) That exemplary damages should be awarded if, but only if, they considered that the compensation awarded by way of basic and aggravated damages was in the circumstances an inadequate punishment for the defendants.

(c) That an award of exemplary damages was in effect a windfall for the plaintiff and, where damages would be payable out of police funds, the sum awarded might not be available to be expended by the police in a way which would benefit the public. That guidance would not be appropriate if the claim was to be met by insurers.

(d) That the sum awarded by way of exemplary damages should be sufficient to mark the jury's disapproval of the oppressive or arbitrary behaviour but should be no more than was required for that purpose.

13 Where exemplary damages were appropriate they were unlikely to be less than £5,000. Otherwise the case was probably not one which justified an award of exemplary damages at all.

The conduct had to be particularly deserving of condemnation for an award of as much as £25,000 to be justified and the figure of £50,000 should be regarded as the absolute maximum, involving directly officers of at least the rank of superintendent.

14 In an appropriate case the jury should also be told that even though the plaintiff succeeded on liability any improper conduct of which they found him guilty could reduce or even eliminate any award of aggravated or

exemplary damages if the jury considered that that conduct caused or contributed to the behaviour complained of.

Public Interest Immunity Certificates

The pre-trial procedures in civil cases differ from those of the criminal courts. There is a variation between High Court and county court procedures but the principles are the same.

The procedure starts by the issue of a writ or summons on behalf of the plaintiff who gives an outline of the nature of the claim, including the facts on which the claim is based. Neither evidence or law is detailed at this time. The defendant then makes his main pleading to admit or refute the claim and may even make a counter-claim to which the plaintiff will have to make a reply.

Following this, either party can require further and better particulars of the claim and later there may be a requirement for the *discovery of documents* or *interrogatories*. Discovery of documents means the other party must produce specified documents for examination of the requesting party and interrogatories are written questions that must be answered on oath by one of the parties. The foregoing are included in what are called the *interlocutory matters* which are designed to save all possible time in court and also to prevent either side from introducing surprise evidence at the trial.

The Crown may claim that it is against the public interest to disclose some documents and may under the *privilege* of the royal prerogative issue a Public Interest Immunity Certificate. The Home Secretary would sign such a certificate in respect of any particular police document.

Lord Bingham said in relation to public interest immunity certificates:

> Where a litigant asserts that the documents are immune from production or disclosure on public interest grounds he is not (if the claim is well founded) claiming a right but observing a duty. Public interest immunity is not a trump card vouchsafed to certain privileged players to play when and as they wish.

It was reported in the press (*Mail on Sunday*, 20 March 1994) as follows:

> The former Deputy Chief Constable of the Ministry of Defence Police (Norman Chapple) had refused to hand over documents to an MOD policeman charged with a disciplinary offence on the grounds that they were covered by public interest immunity. The absence of the document, a statement made by another MOD police officer who was found to have lied on several occasions, prevented adequate cross-examination of the witness and therefore denied the complainant justice.

> The High Court held that Chapple had no authority to claim public interest immunity without having a certificate signed and issued by the secretary of state.

There is a wide range of documents covered by this form of privilege, from the point of view of the police. The following have been declared to be 'immune' documents in court judgments [emphasis added].

Documents relating to the investigation of crime

Evans v Chief Constable of Surrey (1988)

A report sent by a chief constable to the Director of Public Prosecutions, in the course of a murder investigation was covered. It **could not be disclosed** in a later civil claim for damages against the police for wrongful imprisonment.

O'Sullivan v Commissioner of Police of the Metropolis (1995)

The initial report form sent by the police to the Crown Prosecution Service, following an investigation into a suspected criminal offence, belonged to a class of documents to which **public interest immunity attached**.

Documents relating to police operational planning and training

Gill and another v Chief Constable of Lancashire (1992)

A police public order manual is protected from disclosure at trial unless the party seeking disclosure establishes that he cannot properly present his case without it.

R v Sefton Justices ex parte Sharples (1992)

A Police Manual of General Instructions is likewise **protected from disclosure**.

Documents relating to personnel records

Conway v Rimmer (1968)

This case involved an ex police probationer who was dismissed as unlikely to become a good and efficient police officer following an unsuccessful prosecution for theft. He alleged malicious prosecution against the Superintendent concerned and sought discovery of his probationer reports including the report from the police training centre. **The House of Lords rejected the claim of privilege and ordered that the documents be produced.**

Documents relating to complaints, disciplinary and grievance proceedings

Neilson v Laugharne (1980)

Statements taken by police for the purpose of investigating complaints against other members of the police force, are, in respect of the subject matter of the complaint, in civil actions against the police **subject to immunity**.

Police Complaints Authority v Greater Manchester Police Authority (1990)

This case involved a letter from the Police Complaints Authority to a complainant setting out the results of the Authority's investigation. Greater Manchester Police Authority acquired a copy of the letter in error and decided to publish it ostensibly as part of its function as the Force's disciplinary supervisor.

The court made a declaration that the letter was confidential to the PCA and made an injunction restraining the Police Authority from publishing it.

R v Chief Constable of West Midlands ex parte Willey (1993)
R v Chief Constable of Nottinghamshire ex parte Sunderland (1993)

The House of Lords concurred with the *Neilson v Laugharne* judgment but added that **the immunity extends to restrict the use of information in the documents in civil proceedings, and not merely the disclosure of the documents.** (This means that police cannot use the information in such documents in support of their own case.)

Thorpe v Chief Constable of Greater Manchester (1989)

Findings of guilt against police officers in police disciplinary proceedings are not discoverable in a civil action against the police officers since those findings would lead solely to cross-examination as to credit and would not have a material bearing on the issues to be decided in the action.

R v Bromell, Re Coventry Evening Telegraph (1992)

The Court of Appeal held that the **public interest in the confidentiality of evidence given to an internal police disciplinary investigation could be outweighed by a public interest in limited disclosure of such evidence to enable justice to be done** in a defamation action brought by the officers whose conduct had been investigated.

Taylor v Anderton (Police Complaints Authority) (1995)

This case related to the production of the reports made by the investigating officer into complaints made about police conduct. The reports included the opinions of the investigating officers on the veracity of the evidence recorded.

The Court of Appeal held that **in any given case a trial judge could rule in favour of disclosure if the balance of public interest favoured this, but initially the presumption would be against disclosure.**

Commissioner of Police of the Metropolis v Locker (1993)

Public interest immunity does not attach to statements generated in the course of the Metropolitan Police **grievance procedure** and such statements are therefore not immune to disclosure.

In 1995, John Stalker, erstwhile Deputy Chief Constable of Greater Manchester Police was banned from giving some evidence in a civil case. The public interest immunity certificate was signed by the Secretary of State for Northern Ireland and related to matters that Stalker had been involved with in Northern Ireland.

16 The Law of Tort and the Police

The scope of tort

The law of tort deals with people's obligations towards each other – to refrain from harming others, or, if harm has been done, to either repair it or compensate for it. The purpose of this law is to shift any loss sustained by the victim to the person who caused, or was responsible for it. It also gives victims the opportunity to claim compensation for non-financial harms that have been suffered.

The person who commits a tort is called a *tortfeasor*.

The plaintiff must prove that the defendant was responsible, in legal terms, for the harm he suffered. If the plaintiff is found to be wholly, or partly, to blame for the harm he suffered, any damages awarded may be reduced in proportion to his degree of blameworthiness. The standard of proof is based upon the balance of probabilities rather than the strict level of proof needed to convict someone in a criminal court.

Not all harm suffered by an individual is actionable in the courts. If an event is:

- an inevitable accident;
- an act of God;
- an action justified in law

there is no legal course of action open to the victim. This was emphasised in the High Court by Judge David Clarke (*The Times*, 23 April 1997) when he said:

> This action seems to be an example of the increasingly common public feeling that, for every misfortune, somebody must be to blame. This is not so. There is still such a thing as an unfortunate accident for which nobody can be held liable.

Tort actions against the police

It is now fairly commonplace for a person who feels that he has been wronged by the police to take action in the civil courts. Following are the main forms of action that are most likely to affect police officers.

Trespass to the person

Trespass to the person consists of the torts of assault, battery and false imprisonment.

Assault and battery

The torts of assault and battery overlap the criminal law and they have similar definitions.

An assault is an unlawful attempt or threat of applying force or violence to another person with the intention of implementing the threat. The application of force is not necessary for the assault to be completed. A battery is the actual use of force on another person and this includes any hostile touching no matter how slight it is.

Police, during the performance of their duties, will habitually use force to restrain wrongdoers, but when this is done in accordance with the Police and Criminal Evidence Act 1984 it is not unlawful.

Claims of unlawful assaults by police officers are usually conjoined with other torts and so there are few cases that examine the question of assaults by police officers as single issues. In most of these cases there is abundant evidence of the force used, the question at issue is whether its use was justifiable in the circumstance of the incident. Cases of interest are:

Collins v Wilcock (1984)

A woman police officer touched a woman deliberately, but without an intention to do more than restrain her temporarily. The police action was unlawful because the woman had the legal right not to be restrained and the touching was therefore deemed to be hostile.

R v Constanza (1997)

In this case the Court of Appeal held that in order to prove that an assault had been committed, it was enough to prove a fear of violence at some time not excluding the immediate future. An assault could be committed by words alone.

False imprisonment

This tort is committed when the defendant intentionally and directly places a total restraint upon the liberty of the plaintiff. It does not require a physical act aimed against the person of the plaintiff and imprisonment by a show of authority, by, for example, a police officer, is sufficient. The tort can be committed by making a wrongful arrest, by detaining someone for longer than is justifiable or simply by preventing someone from leaving a room.

Note that there is no such tort as *wrongful arrest*. A plaintiff may prove a *prima facie* false imprisonment and/or a battery by proving the facts of his unlawful (or wrongful) arrest. The burden of proof then switches to the defendant to establish the defence of lawful arrest in conformity with the Police and Criminal Evidence Act 1984.

Meering v Graham White Aviation Co (1919)

The plaintiff was suspected of stealing some varnish from the defendant's factory. He was taken to the company's offices where two works policemen remained close to him whilst he was questioned. The defendant argued that the plaintiff was unaware that he had been imprisoned and so it was impossible for the tort to have been committed.

Held that a person could be imprisoned without his knowing it. A person could be imprisoned while he is asleep, while he is in a state of drunkenness, while he is unconscious, and while he is a lunatic. The damages might be diminished and would be affected by the question whether he was conscious of it or not.

Murray v Ministry of Defence (1988)

The House of Lords confirmed the Meering judgment and Lord Griffiths said:

> ... the law attaches supreme importance to the liberty of the individual and if he suffers a wrongful interference with that liberty it should remain actionable even without proof of special damage.

Hill v Chief Constable of South Yorkshire Police (1989)

The plaintiff was arrested at 2.40 am and detained until 5.15 am when he was charged with being drunk and disorderly and released. At the court hearing he pleaded guilty and was fined. He claimed wrongful arrest and detention because the police, in breach of the Police and Criminal Evidence Act 1984 had failed to inform him of the reason for his arrest, and, he was unlawfully detained because he should have been released on bail as soon as the officer had sufficient evidence to charge him.

Held that a plaintiff who had pleaded guilty to an offence was not thereby prevented from bringing a claim for wrongful arrest or wrongful detention. The plea would be relevant if the arrest was challenged as being made without reasonable grounds for suspicion and could not affect a challenge to the arrest and detention based on statutory requirements for establishing the lawfulness of arrest or detention.

The onus would lie upon the chief constable to produce evidence that the Police and Criminal Evidence Act 1984 had been complied with and thus demonstrate that no cause of action lay with the plaintiff.

Plange v Chief Constable of South Humberside Police (1992)

In this case the victim of an assault had told the police that the plaintiff was the assailant but later stated that he did not wish to pursue the complaint as the assailant had apologised. The plaintiff was arrested and detained at the police station for four hours and released without charge.

Lord Justice Parker said that it was conceded that the police officer had reasonable grounds for the arrest and the force used was reasonable. Under these circumstances the action of the arresting officer could only be challenged if he knew that there was no possibility of a charge being made. However, an uncommunicated decision made at headquarters not to charge the suspect could not make the arrest itself unlawful. Under these circumstances there was sufficient evidence for the case to go to the jury to consider whether, at the time of the arrest, the arresting officer knew that there was no possibility of a charge and had therefore acted on some irrelevant consideration or for an improper reason.

Davidson v Chief Constable of North Wales Police (1993)

In this case a store detective incorrectly told police officers that the plaintiff had been shoplifting and she was arrested on the basis of this information. She was not charged and it was accepted that she was entirely innocent of any dishonesty. The plaintiff sued the defendant store detective for damages in respect of false imprisonment. The claim was dismissed and the case was appealed.

It was held that the defendant store detective was not liable for false imprisonment for merely giving information to the police and the police had effected the plaintiff's arrest and detention. The defendant store detective had neither instigated nor procured the arrest. Although the store detective in question expected her information to carry weight with the police, who had always acted upon it, and she regarded the arrest as being made on her behalf, the police officers had exercised their own judgment in making the arrest.

However, the situation is different if the informant maliciously gives the police false information, as in:

Austin v Dowling (1870)

In this case the informant had locked his lodger out of his room following a dispute over the payment of rent and the lodger subsequently forced his way into the room to recover his personal property. The landlord detained the lodger and told the police that the man was a burglar so he was taken to the police station. At the police station the landlord informant was required to sign the charge sheet to accept responsibility for the arrest. Later the facts of the case emerged and it was held that the police were not liable for false imprisonment, the responsibility lay with the informant.

[See also *Martin v Watson* (1995), re malicious prosecution on page 143.]

Hyland v Chief Constable of Lancashire Constabulary (1996)

Actions against the police for false imprisonment and breach of statutory duty could not be taken by a detainee for alleged unnecessary detention after he had been remanded in custody to a police station by a magistrates' court.

Olotu v Secretary of State for the Home Department and another (1996)

In this case a remand prisoner remained in custody after the expiry of the time limit through the failure of the Crown Prosecution Service to apply for its extension and the prisoner did not apply for bail.

The Court of Appeal held that there was no right of action against the Home Office for false imprisonment or against the Crown Prosecution Service for breach of a statutory duty.

It was reported in the press (*The Times*, 12 June 1996) that Simon Wild, a hunt saboteur, was awarded £500 by Sussex Police after threatening action against the Force for 'wrongful arrest'. Wild had made four previous claims against police forces, all of which were settled out of court for a total of about £5,000.

Malicious prosecution

McDonagh and another v Commissioner of Police for the Metropolis (1989)

The tort of malicious prosecution has four elements, all of which the plaintiff has to prove:

(1) that he was prosecuted;

(2) that he was acquitted;

(3) there was an absence of reasonable and probable cause for the prosecution; and

(4) there was malice.

If he was unable to prove (3) then the fact that he could prove malice did not of itself entitle him to succeed in an alternative claim based on the tort of misfeasance in a public office.

Martin v Watson (1995)

A complaint was made to the police that the plaintiff had indecently exposed himself. He was arrested and charged but in court the prosecution offered no evidence and the charge was dismissed.

As the original complainant had falsely and maliciously complained, and the facts were solely within her knowledge, the police could not have exercised any independent discretion, therefore the (police) prosecutor could not be sued. The original complainant in this case could be sued for malicious prosecution.

Misfeasance in a public office

This tort was defined in:

Racz v Home Office (1992)

In the Court of Appeal Lord Neill said:

> The deliberate abuse of power by a person holding a public office was tortious. In order to establish an actionable tort it was necessary to prove either:
>
> 1 that the officer or authority knew that it did not possess the power to take the action in question; or
>
> 2 that the officer or authority was actuated by malice, for example, by personal spite or a desire to injure for improper reasons.

[This case went on to the House of Lords where the issue of vicarious liability was decided, see pages 24 and 128.]

Three Rivers District Council and others v Bank of England (1996)

A plaintiff had a sufficient interest to maintain an action of misfeasance in public office at common law where it was established:

1 that the defendant was a public officer who intended to injure him and knew he had no power to do what he did and that the plaintiff would probably suffer loss; and

2 that the plaintiff had suffered loss as a result of the wrongful act.

Silcott v Commissioner of Police of the Metropolis (1996)

A person whose conviction for a crime was subsequently quashed on the ground that it was unsafe and unsatisfactory could not bring any civil action for conspiracy to pervert the course of justice and misfeasance in public office against police officers investigating the crime who, he alleged, had created a false record of an incriminating interview with him, because the officers were protected by a rule of absolute immunity conferred as a matter of public policy. (See the *Hill* case on pages 148–49.)

Elliott v Chief Constable of Wiltshire and others (1996)

A person who had suffered damage when a policeman, holding himself out as a police officer, had disclosed that person's previous convictions for an improper purpose and with intent to cause him injury, arguably had a remedy in damages against the police officer for the tort of misfeasance in public office.

Police officers had a status that was the source of important powers and duties. If they were guilty of misconduct and the other ingredients of the tort (malice, intent to injure, improper purpose and damage) were present the tort of misfeasance in public office would be made out.

Breach of statutory duty

This is a civil action brought against a person for failing to comply with a statutory duty laid down in criminal law. To justify the action the plaintiff must show that:

- the statute was intended by Parliament to confer a civil remedy for its breach;
- that the statute imposed a duty upon the defendant;
- that the defendant was in breach of this duty; and
- that the plaintiff suffered harm or damage which was a consequence of the breach of duty and which was not too remote.

When an Act of Parliament imposing a duty provides no remedy if that duty is breached then there may be a cause of action for tort. If the Act itself contains remedies for breaches of its own provisions then it would be difficult to show that an action in tort would lie.

This matter is examined in an article entitled 'Public authorities and damages claims' published in *The Times*, 18 July 1995 by David Pannick, QC. Pannick gives details relating to this topic and says:

Just because a public authority has breached a public law duty does not of itself entitle the complainant to damages. A claim for damages must be based on a private law cause of action.

- Damages will be awarded where the public authority is guilty of misfeasance in public office, that is, where it acts with the intention of injuring the plaintiff or in the knowledge that its conduct is unlawful.

- Damages are available where the public authority is in breach of a statutory duty which was designed to confer a private right of action for damages.

- Damages may be claimed where the public authority has acted negligently in performing statutory functions. Such a claim cannot succeed if the alleged negligence is in the exercise of a statutory discretion involving policy decisions by the public body, or concerns a decision within the scope of the discretion conferred by Parliament.

Breach of confidence

Breach of confidence is a tort used to provide protection against the disclosure or use of information that the owner has not placed in the public domain. The information has been entrusted by the owner in circumstances that impose an obligation not to disclose it without authorisation from the person who originally provided it. Virtually all information gathered by police during the course of their duties can be categorised as confidential information in these terms.

If an individual constable makes improper use or disclosure of confidential information then he may be subjected to criminal and/or disciplinary proceedings, see 'Misuse of police computer data', page 25 and 'Other discipline matters', page 118.

Circumstances may arise when, after due deliberation, a chief constable deems it in the public interest to disclose confidential information without the authorisation of the person concerned. Such disclosures may be challenged in the courts.

Hellewell v Chief Constable of Derbyshire (1995)

In this case the plaintiff was photographed following arrest for theft; he had 19 previous convictions. The photograph, and others, were circulated to local shopkeepers to help in identifying potential offenders.

Hellewell brought an action for breach of confidence on the grounds that the photograph had been taken without his consent and any distribution was therefore unlawful. Police applied for Hellewell's action to be struck out on the basis that it disclosed no reasonable cause of action as they had been acting in the furtherance of their obligation to prevent and detect crime.

Laws J, said that to distribute a photograph taken in these circumstances could be actionable unless the police could provide evidence to show that they had acted in the public interest. In this case they had acted reasonably and in good faith to prevent the commission of crimes, to assist in the investigation of offences and to assist in the apprehension of offenders. The action was struck out.

R v Chief Constable of North Wales Police and others ex parte AB and another (1997)

This case related to two paedophile offenders who after completion of a term of imprisonment eventually took up residence at a caravan site. The police were concerned for the safety of children expected to holiday at the site and after high level discussions, revealed details of the convictions to the site owner. The owner then directed the applicants to move, which they did.

The court cited the policy principles included in the Home Secretary's guide to the police in such cases.

• A general presumption that information should not be disclosed.

• A strong public interest existed in ensuring that police could disclose information about offenders where it was necessary for the prevention or detection of crime or for the protection of young or other vulnerable people.

• Each case should be considered on its own facts, assessing the risk by the offender, the vulnerability of those at risk and the impact of disclosure on the offender.

The court accepted these principles and cited authorities that supported them.

It was accepted that as convictions and sentences had been formally announced in open court such information was in the public domain and not subject to a duty of confidence, nonetheless, it was said, a general policy of disclosure could never be justified.

It was not acceptable that those who had undergone the lawful punishment imposed by the courts should be the subject of intimidation and private vengeance, harried from parish to parish like paupers under the old Poor Law. However, in this case the North Wales Police policy and conduct fell within the bounds of legality and the application was dismissed.

It has been said that the applicant will appeal against this decision of the Queen's Bench Divisional Court.

Negligence actions

The tort of negligence is the breach of a legal duty of care which results in damage, to the plaintiff. Negligence is either:

* the failure to do something which a reasonable person, guided by ordinary considerations, would do; or
* doing what a prudent and reasonable person would not do.

The defining precedent for all subsequent negligence actions was made in 1932 in the following case:

Donoghue v Stevenson (1932)

Lord Atkin said:

> The rule that you are to love your neighbour becomes, in law, you must not injure your neighbour; and the lawyer's question, 'Who is my neighbour?' receives a restricted reply. You must take reasonable care to avoid acts or omissions which you can reasonably foresee would be likely to injure your neighbour. Who then, in law is my neighbour? The answer seems to be – persons who are so closely and directly affected by my act that I ought reasonably to have them in contemplation as being so affected when I am directing my mind to the acts or omissions which are called in question.

In law negligent conduct is not the same as deliberate conduct, because the person offending does not intend the harm that results from his action. In ordinary terms it is failing to look for the consequences of an action that could harm someone.

Negligence is a common law tort which, since 1932, has been examined in courts at all levels. Decisions have been made on virtually every aspect of negligence and these decisions must be read to ascertain their application in any particular case. In a negligence action the court will consider the questions:

* Does the defendant owe the plaintiff a duty of care?
* Has the defendant breached that duty of care?
* Has the plaintiff suffered damage as a result of the breach of the duty of care?

146

The diagram below, together with the following explanation provide a brief explanation of the major points that have to be proven in any case of negligence.

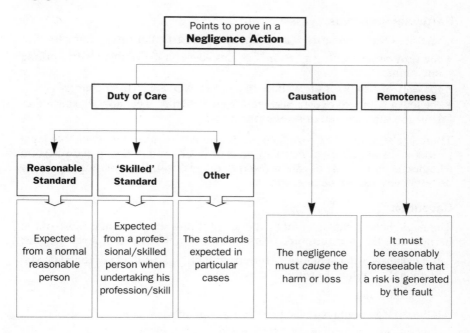

The duty of care

The standard of the duty of care demanded by law is sometimes described as an *objective standard*, this is the standard achieved by most people undertaking the particular task. For example, if a learner driver, driving as carefully as he can, has an accident which a more experienced driver would have avoided, then he will be liable for any injury or damage that results. He will be judged by the standard of care expected from most drivers, not his own incompetent standard. Similarly, the newest police probationer constable will be expected to act to the same standard as a long service constable.

Professional standard of care

In the case of a professional person, such as a doctor or a lawyer the 'reasonable person' in the definition becomes a 'reasonable person learned in the particular profession'. This standard of conduct is, naturally, higher than for a non-professional person and failure to attain it was described by Lord Chief Justice Taylor in 1993 as being gross negligence. He said that the points to be considered by a jury would be:

• indifference to an obvious risk of injury to health;
• lack of foresight of the risk;
• inattention, or failing to avert a serious risk beyond 'mere inadvertence'.

147

Any accidents caused by police actions in the use of, say, firearms, police patrol cars or other hazardous operations for which police officers are specially trained would be judged by this higher standard.

Particular standards

There are other standards of care that apply in particular cases, examples are:

- the duty of an employer towards an employee in providing a safe working environment;
- the duty of adults for the welfare of children who are in their charge;
- the lower standard of care accepted from a child who cannot be expected to have the same degree of foresight as an adult.

There are several other particular cases that can be found in a suitable legal textbook. In many cases the main area of legal conflict lies in the question whether, or not, a duty of care is owed to the plaintiff. If there is no legal duty of care, there cannot be negligence.

Causation

The negligence complained of by the plaintiff must be the actual cause of the harm or loss that was suffered. This has been described in the following terms:

> If the damage would **not** have occurred **but for** the particular fault complained of, then that fault is the cause of the damage,

> on the other hand,

> if the damage would have happened *irrespective* of whether the fault occurred, then the fault complained of is **not** the cause of the damage.

Remoteness

It must be reasonably foreseeable by a reasonable person that a risk might be generated by the fault complained of. However, although the fact that damage is of a kind that should be foreseen by a reasonable man, the extent of that damage does not have to be foreseeable.

Negligence actions instituted against the police

The investigation and suppression of crime

The *Hill* case is the principal case regarding police immunity from liability when engaged in operational matters relating to crime prevention and detection.

Hill v Chief Constable of West Yorkshire (1988)

The mother of Jacqueline Hill (a victim of Sutcliffe, the Yorkshire Ripper) claimed damages for the death of her daughter on the grounds that the Chief Constable and his officers failed to exercise all reasonable care and skill to apprehend Sutcliffe.

The matter was appealed to the House of Lords where it was held that although the police owed a duty to the general public to enforce the criminal law, they could not be liable in damages for negligence to individual members of the public for damage caused by a criminal whom they failed to apprehend.

Osman v Ferguson (1993)

A schoolteacher formed an unhealthy attachment to a 15 year old male pupil and harassed him. The teacher damaged property belonging to the boy's father and he was dismissed from his post but he continued the harassment. The teacher told the police that he was distressed and feared that he would do something criminally insane. Subsequently he deliberately rammed a vehicle in which the boy was travelling as a passenger. Later he shot and severely injured the boy and killed the boy's father. An action was brought against the police for negligence in that they were aware of the teacher's activities but they had failed to apprehend him, interview him or charge him with a serious offence until the time of the shooting.

Held that as the boy and his family had been exposed to a risk over and above that suffered by members of the public, there was an arguable case that there was a close relationship between the plaintiff's family and the investigating police officers. However, for the reasons given in *Hill* and *Alexandrou* it would be against public policy to impose a duty of care on the police, therefore the police would be immune to liability in this case.

It has been reported that Mrs Osman, the widow of the victim, has taken the matter to the European Commission on Human Rights. The Commission has declared that her case of negligence by the police is admissible under Article 2 of the Human Rights Convention (the Right to Life). If the case is successful, police immunity as defined in the *Hill* case might be abolished.

Elguzouli-Daf v Commissioner of Police for the Metropolis (1995)

Public policy immunity might not apply if the Crown Prosecution Service or police voluntarily assume responsibility.

Swinney and another v Chief Constable of Northumbria Police (1996)

This case is of significance in relation to police informants. Although the police as a matter of public policy were in general immune from actions for negligence in respect of their activities in the investigation and suppression of crime, that immunity could be displaced by other considerations of public policy for the protection of the public.

In this case Mr and Mrs Swinney complained of a breach of the duty of confidentiality by police officers. Statements signed by, and identifying the Swinneys, in respect of a violent criminal fell into the hands of that criminal. Subsequently they were threatened with violence and arson and as a result they suffered psychological damage. They were allowed to pursue a negligence suit, as, amongst other things, this was a case in which the police had voluntarily accepted responsibility for ensuring confidentiality.

R v Reading Justices and others ex parte South West Meats Ltd (1991)

The police, when co-operating with other bodies in obtaining and executing a search warrant, should not delegate their powers and duties, including those under the Police and Criminal Evidence Act 1984, to those bodies in an unacceptable manner.

In this case an officer of Avon and Somerset Constabulary obtained a search warrant which was executed in company with officials of the Intervention Board for Agricultural Produce. Subsequently the warrant was declared invalid rendering the consequent search and seizure of documents unlawful. It was conceded by the Board and the police that the warrant was unlawful and that access should have been given to South West Meats at an earlier stage. Damages, including exemplary damages were awarded against the Board and the chief constable.

Prisoners and property

Kirkham v Anderton (1989)

In this case, Kirkham was arrested and police were told at the time that he was a suicide risk. The correct form was not completed and when he was taken to a remand centre he was placed in an ordinary cell instead of being put in the hospital wing. He committed suicide during the night.

The Court of Appeal held that the suicide was caused by the police negligently failing to warn the prison authorities of the prisoner's suicidal tendencies and damages were awarded against them.

Sutcliffe v Chief Constable of West Yorkshire (1995)

The police when acting as bailees were not to be held liable for damage caused by vandals to a motor vehicle held by them in a secure yard under Police and Criminal Evidence Act 1984 powers.

Road traffic matters

Marshall v Osman (1982)

The plaintiff was a passenger in a stolen vehicle that was being chased by the police and was injured by being struck by the police car on alighting from the stolen vehicle. The court found the driver of the police car not liable on the grounds that the same duty of care as that owed to law-abiding citizens was not owed to occupants of a vehicle believed to be stolen and of which the police were in hot pursuit.

The duty in these circumstances is a reduced one and may be limited to abstaining from deliberately injuring the plaintiff.

Topp v London Country Bus (South West) Ltd (1993)

The driver of a minibus left the vehicle parked in a lay-by, the unattended vehicle being unlocked and having the key left in the ignition. The vehicle was subsequently taken by an unidentified person who was involved in an accident in which the plaintiff's wife was killed. The owners of the minibus were sued for negligence in the manner of leaving the vehicle.

The Court of Appeal held that even if the defendants had been at fault in the manner of leaving the minibus, they were still not responsible in law for the voluntary actions of a third party who was completely unknown to them and the claim was dismissed.

Webb v Thomas (1992)

The occasion was a Welsh language demonstration. Mr Webb intended to demonstrate by sitting in front of the official car carrying a government minister, driven by Mr Thomas, and, as the car moved forward, Mr Webb was forced on to the bonnet of the vehicle. Mr Thomas, the driver, could and should have stopped once he found Mr Webb on the bonnet, instead he accelerated and carried Mr Webb a considerable distance before he fell off. This was a further and greater breach of his duty of care as it plainly hazarded Mr Webb's safety and there was no conceivable justification for it. Mr Thomas was found to be 80% to blame for the injuries and was ordered to pay £7,879 in compensation.

Ancell and another v McDermott and others (1993)

Police from one force provided assistance at a road accident and noticed that diesel oil had been spilled on the road but did nothing about it. The plaintiff's wife was killed and the other plaintiffs were injured when their car skidded on the oil.

Held that police officers who come across a hazard on the highway which is a danger to drivers owe no duty of care to drivers to protect them from or warn them against hazards which were created by others or for which the officers were not responsible.

Private premises

Rigby v Chief Constable of Northamptonshire (1985)

In this case the police had fired a canister of CS gas into the premises of the plaintiff in order to flush out a dangerous armed psychopath who had taken refuge there and was feared to present an immediate danger to the public. As a result the premises caught fire and were destroyed.

The police were found to be liable on the ground that they should have delayed firing the canister until fire fighting services were in attendance and they were negligent as they did not so wait.

Alexandrou v Oxford (1990)

An occupier of property protected by a burglar alarm system, which was connected to a police station and which when activated sent a 999 telephone call to the police station did not stand in a special relationship with the police. Accordingly the police did not owe him a duty of care and are not liable in negligence if he suffers loss from a burglary.

Personal injury

Claims have been made against the police in respect of personal injury, most usually as a result of road traffic accidents. However, there are no particular points that differentiate such claims from other accident claims.

See *Hicks and others v Chief Constable of South Yorkshire Police* (1992) on page 153.

Nervous shock

The duty of care in relation to the condition called nervous shock was first recognised in 1901 and since then the extent of the duty has been extended in a series of decisions.

This condition has been described by psychiatrists as post traumatic stress disorder (PTSD). It is a condition that occurs as a result of a particular incident, although an individual might experience several traumatic incidents before succumbing to it. The medical title is based upon the definitions as follows:

Trauma – An emotional shock following a stressful event, sometimes leading to long-term neurosis.

Neurosis – A mental illness characterised by irrational or depressive thought or behaviour caused by a disorder of the nervous system, usually without organic change

In April 1989 there occurred a disastrous event at Hillsborough football ground when, through overcrowding in part of the ground, 96 spectators were killed and over 400 injured. It was subsequently claimed that the deaths and injuries were attributable to the negligence of the police and the owners of the football ground and to this end several claims were instigated, mostly relating to the nervous shock suffered by the claimants. Two cases in particular went on appeal to the House of Lords which demonstrated the gravity and public concern over the events.

Alcock v Chief Constable of South Yorkshire (1991)

This case was instituted by relatives of victims who claimed that they had suffered *nervous shock* as a result of the events at Hillsborough. Their Lordships reviewed all of the previous law relating to claims of this nature and made a definitive statement of the law as it stood. The main points are best illustrated by the diagram below:

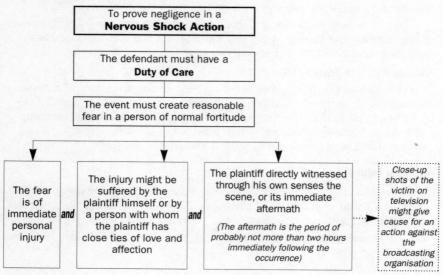

These claims all failed for one or more of the following reasons:

- Those present at the ground were too far away to be able to observe the faces of victims at close quarters.
- Those who saw the event on television did not see details of the faces of individual victims as they were not broadcast.
- One claimant who identified his brother eight hours later in the mortuary fell outside the terms of the 'immediate aftermath'.

A later claim in respect of the same incident also went to the House of Lords:

Hicks and others v Chief Constable of South Yorkshire Police (1992)

These claims were made on behalf of the estates of three deceased victims from Hillsborough. The basis of the claim was that the three victims who had died from traumatic asphyxia had suffered mental agony and pain before unconsciousness and death occurred. It was asserted that this was caused by the negligence of the police officers at the scene.

The claim was disallowed on the grounds that the last few moments of mental agony and pain were in reality part of the death itself. The action had been brought under the Law Reform (Miscellaneous Provisions) Act 1934 and the court found that no damages were payable under the terms of that Act.

It was reported in the press (*The Times*, 12 December 1996) that the half-brother of one of the victims, who was present at the ground at the time of the occurrence was awarded damages in the High Court. The judge was reported as saying 'I have considered the matter most anxiously, as I am well aware that the House of Lords indicated the limitations on this type of claim. My decision creates no precedent'. No doubt the claim was within the parameters laid down in *Alcock*.

Negligence actions instituted against fire brigades

Constables, by the nature of their duties, undertake life and property saving tasks in the absence of specialists such as firemen. Actions of this sort do not relate to a constable's peace-keeping role and consequently the immunity to liability as defined in the *Hill* judgment would not be applicable. Some of the following cases could be relevant.

Duff v Highland and Islands Fire Board (1995)

The House of Lords held that a fire brigade did not, in operational matters, enjoy an immunity for negligence analogous to that which protected the police in relation to the investigation and suppression of crime.

The following three appeal cases were heard together in the Court of Appeal as they all related to claims of negligence by fire brigades when attending to fires.

1 Capital and Counties plc and another v Hampshire County Council (1997)

2 John Monroe (Acrylics) Ltd v London Fire and Civil Defence Authority and others (1997)

3 Church of Jesus Christ of Latter-Day Saints (Great Britain) v Yorkshire Fire and Civil Defence Authority (1997)

Following were the brief facts in each case:

1 Whilst attending a fire, a fire officer ordered that a sprinkler system should be turned off. This action had an adverse effect in controlling the fire.

2 A company involved in film special effects caused a deliberate explosion and burning debris was scattered over a wide area. Some burning debris fell on the plaintiff's premises. Fire Brigade officers checked to ensure that all fires had been extinguished then left the scene without inspecting the plaintiff's property. Later that evening a fire broke out at the plaintiff's premises causing severe damage.

3 The Fire Brigade arrived at a fire at the plaintiff's chapel but could not fight the fire due to the absence of a proper supply of water.

The Court of Appeal held that a fire brigade is not under a common law duty to answer a call for help or take care to do so, but, there was a liability in negligence if they made the situation worse and thus caused the plaintiff injury. In these cases the Fire Brigade in case 1 was found to be negligent in making the fire worse and they were ordered to pay damages. In cases 2 and 3 it was held that the Fire Brigades did not have a duty of care in the circumstances of the respective cases.

The above cases were cited in a subsequent negligence action against the coastguard:

OII Ltd v Secretary of State for the Home Department (1997)

The coastguard owed no duty of care where it negligently misdirected its own personnel or equipment while trying to rescue people in danger at sea nor did it owe a duty of care where it misdirected people outside its own service.

17   Constables as Plaintiffs

There are circumstances where police officers could be plaintiffs rather than defendants in negligence actions.

Personal injury

Claims against third parties

The first important case in this field was:

Haynes v Harwood (1935)

In this case a policeman was injured when he attempted to stop the defendant's runaway horses from injuring other persons.

It was held that the policeman had a general duty to protect the life and property of inhabitants and had a right to recover damages from the defendant whose servant's negligence resulted in the horses being runaways.

The policeman was entitled to recover damages because he was endeavouring to save the people in danger from death or injury.

The *Haynes* case above was cited in a fire brigade case of importance:

Ogwo v Taylor (1987)

This was a House of Lords' decision in which it was held that a person who negligently started a fire was liable in damages to a professional fireman who, doing no more and no less than his proper duty, and acting with skill and efficiency in fighting an ordinary fire, was injured by one of the risks to which the particular circumstances of the fire gave rise. The 'rescue' principle was as fully applicable as if other human beings were in immediate jeopardy when the fire was being fought.

The above view of the law was emphasised in the criminal court in June 1997. A security guard named Martin Cody on his first day at work in a Bristol supermarket deliberately set fire to the store. The Fire Brigade attended and whilst engaged in fire fighting operations Fire Officer Fleur Lombard was engulfed in a fireball and killed. Cody was convicted of manslaughter.

A Scottish case related to an injury accidentally received by a police officer on duty at a football match had the following outcome:

Gillon v Chief Constable of Strathclyde Police and another (1996)

There was a foreseeable risk that a police constable watching the spectators at a football match would be injured by a player who was impelled off the pitch in the course of the game, but the risk was so small that a reasonable man would not guard against it. In any event, it would be unreasonable to require the proprietors of the football ground to erect a barrier between the players and the pitchside track. Neither the chief constable nor the proprietor of the ground was held liable.

There were various press reports in January 1997 regarding a road traffic accident involving a police car pursuing a stolen vehicle. The essence of the reports was:

During a high speed chase the police car hit some ice on the road and collided with a lamp post causing severe injuries to the police driver. In the High Court it was held that a duty of care was owed to the police officer and 'if by careless or reckless driving he creates circumstances in which he should see he would be pursued in a manner in which he incurs the risk of injury to the police officer or any other road users, then the defendant is liable'. The judge was also quoted as saying that it was a 'powerful reason' to uphold the constable's claim as police officers should be encouraged to perform their duty in pursuing criminals without fearing that, if injured, they would be without effective remedy.

The damages in this case will be paid by the insurers and they have indicated that they may appeal against this decision.

In 1990 London Underground accepted liability for negligence in the King's Cross fire disaster of 1987 and paid out of court compensation to four fire fighters suffering post traumatic stress disorder. In another case, whilst accepting liability, they challenged the amount of compensation claimed by the fire officer. The High Court subsequently found in the fire fighter's favour.

Claims against employer

In June 1996, 14 police officers who were traumatised at the Hillsborough stadium disaster were awarded a total of £1.2 million in an out of court settlement with liability having been admitted by the chief constable. This settlement related to police officers who had entered the pens or had been active at the fence.

Claims were also made by other police officers in respect of the same event and they later went to court. The subsequent Court of Appeal judgment confirmed that employees and rescuers are owed a specific duty of care that differs from the general duty of care expressed in the *Alcock* case.

Frost and others v Chief Constable of South Yorkshire Police and others (1996)

Liability for the deaths and injuries of the spectators was admitted by the defendants, the first of whom was the plaintiffs' chief constable. The defendants admitted negligence but disputed the existence of any duty to the plaintiffs. It was not in issue that the plaintiffs all sustained post traumatic stress disorder.

Two grounds for founding liability were argued on appeal: first, breach of duty of care by the chief constable, arising from the plaintiffs' service as police officers when acting under his direction and control; second, breach of a duty owed to them as rescuers. The plaintiffs were directly involved in the course of their employment and in the consequences flowing from their employer's negligence they were primary victims.

If fire fighters could not be at any disadvantage in relation to compensation for injury (*Ogwo v Taylor* (1988)) there was no reason why police officers should be at a disadvantage. Among the factors to be considered, although none was in itself decisive, were the following:

- the character and extent of the initial incident caused by the tortfeasor;
- whether that incident was finished or was continuing;
- whether there was any danger, continuing or otherwise, to the victim or to the plaintiff;
- the character of the plaintiff's conduct, in itself and in relation to the victim; and
- how proximate, in time and place, the plaintiff's conduct was to the incident.

In none of the cases before the House of Lords since *Ogwo v Taylor* was the plaintiff either a servant of the defendant or a rescuer. That was a crucial matter which explained why some of the present plaintiffs might succeed where the plaintiffs in *Alcock v Chief Constable of South Yorkshire Police* failed.

The distinction was not due to any preference being given by the courts to police officers over laypersons. It existed because the court had long recognised a duty of care to guard employees and rescuers against all kinds of injury, whereas in deciding whether any duty of care existed towards plaintiffs who were not employees, rescuers, or primary victims, the courts had, in recent years, imposed specific criteria in relation to claims for psychiatric injury.

Henry, LJ said that while the duty of care to the police officers was a factor in a case such as this where their employer had been negligent, he would expect a duty to be owed to them by any defendant who caused such a disaster. Deterrence was part of the public policy behind tort law. Prevention was better than cure and potential defendants should face up to their safety responsibilities before rather than after an accident.

Where a plaintiff was a direct victim because of the duty that either his employer or the tortfeasor owed to him, that should be the first head of recovery to be considered, because it might be wider and would not be narrower than any entitlement as a rescuer.

Dealing with the entitlement as a rescuer, it seemed to him that public policy favoured a wide rather than a narrow definition, to ensure that those brave and unselfish enough to go to the rescue of their fellow men would be properly compensated as a result.

Finally, he was aware that many people regarded it as unjust that the police should recover damages for post traumatic stress disorder sustained on that terrible day while the relatives claiming in *Alcock* failed. While respecting the relatives' feelings of disappointment that their claim failed, the court could only consider whether the plaintiffs should recover on the different principles of law applicable to them.

The points can be illustrated as:

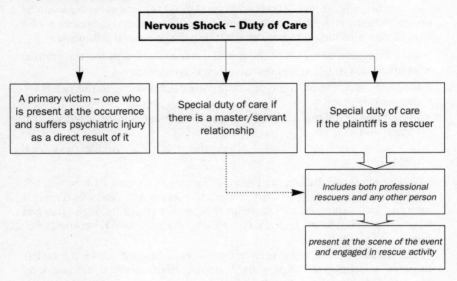

It was reported (*Daily Mail*, 16 June 1997) that the Chief Constable of South Yorkshire Police has been granted leave to appeal to the House of Lords against the above decision by the Court of Appeal.

The Court of Appeal examined the duty of care owed by the chief officer to constables under his command in another case:

W v Commissioner of Police of the Metropolis (1997)

In this case a woman constable had made a complaint that she suffered a sexual assault by a fellow constable in the section house where she was living. She claimed that she suffered mental illness as a result of her treatment by senior officers in the manner of their responses to her complaints.

The court referred to *Calveley* (1989) (see page 161) and stated that the allegations of negligence could not be upheld. The internal affairs of police forces were closely regulated by statute. There was no duty of care which enabled individual officers to claim damages for the negligent performance of those duties.

As the claim was not of negligence in operational circumstances, the Commissioner could not be vicariously liable for the negligence of other officers under his direction and control.

See also 'Vicarious liability', page 127.

Occupational health and safety

The legislation covering these matters is illustrated thus:

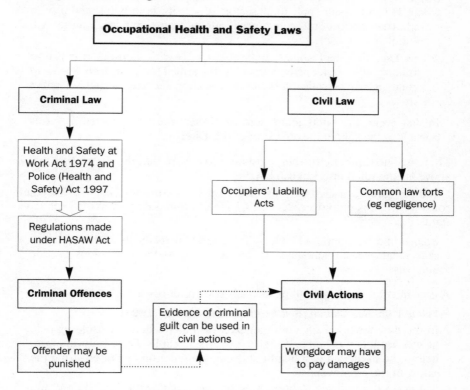

The Health and Safety at Work Act 1974 was not applicable to serving police officers because they are not, in legal terms, employees. However, for the purposes of the 1974 Act, and regulations made thereunder, the chief constable is now deemed to be the employer of constables (section 1 Police (Health and Safety) Act 1997). This means that the chief constable is required to provide safe and healthy working conditions in more or less the same way as any other employer.

This change has been brought about as the government takes steps to implement Council Directive 89/391 of the European Union.

The full scope of health and safety law is outside the range of this handbook, but the following points are of significance.

Article 2 of Directive 89/391 states:

Scope

1 This Directive shall apply to all sectors of activity, both public and private (industrial, agricultural, commercial, administrative, service, educational, cultural, leisure, etc).

2 This Directive shall not be applicable where characteristics peculiar to certain specific service activities, such as the armed forces or the police, or to certain specific activities in the civil protection services inevitably conflict with it.

In that event, the safety and health of workers must be ensured as far as possible in the light of the objectives of this Directive.

There will no doubt be further legislation to ensure that the derogation in 2.2 above is embodied into English law.

With regard to a civil actions instituted by a constable against his chief constable, as his employer, section 47 Health and Safety at Work Act 1974 states:

Breach of a duty imposed by health and safety regulations shall, so far as it causes damage, be actionable except in so far as the regulations provide otherwise.

A case illustrating the extent of such a breach of duty was:

Young v Charles Church (Southern) Ltd and another (1997)

In this case a worker on a building site was killed when a scaffolding pole he was holding touched a 33,000 volt overhead cable. The employers were held to be in breach of a health and safety regulation by not ensuring the safety of the employee.

A second employee, Young, was six feet away from the incident and subsequently suffered psychiatric illness as a direct result of witnessing the event. His claim was originally rejected, but the Court of Appeal held that protection was given, not only to the deceased victim, but to others likely to be endangered – in this case the plaintiff was fortunate to escape electrocution himself.

The statute gives protection to employees from the kinds of injury that can be foreseen as being likely to occur and a breach of statutory duty had occurred in this case.

Occupiers' liability

The occupier of any premises has a duty of care towards all lawful visitors to his premises by virtue of the Occupiers' Liability Acts. The duty is to take reasonable care to ensure that the visitor is safe whilst he is using the premises for the purposes of his visit. The occupier's duty of care towards a constable entering into premises to fulfil his functions is part of the same general duty.

An occupier does not owe the same duty of care to a trespasser as he owes to a lawful visitor. However, he must act by standards of common sense and humanity and warn or exclude, within reasonable limits, those likely to be injured by a known danger.

Police cases of relevance are:

Cunningham and others v Reading Football Club Ltd (1991)

A football club, which failed to maintain the concrete structure of its ground when it knew or ought to have known of the probability that visiting hooligans would, if they could, break off pieces of concrete to use as missiles, could be held liable in negligence and under the Occupiers' Liability Act 1957 for injuries caused by such missiles to other visitors, such as policemen controlling the crowd.

A press report (*The Mail on Sunday*, 8 October 1995):

A policewoman answered a 999 call regarding an alleged intruder at the house of a disabled man. She walked out of the French windows without seeing the wheelchair ramp and slipped on its surface suffering back and arm injuries and concussion. She claimed against the householder under the terms of the Occupiers' Liability Acts and was awarded £2,100 in damages.

Disciplinary matters

Calveley and others v Chief Constable of Merseyside (1989)
Worral and others v Chief Constable of Merseyside (1989)
Park and others v Chief Constable of Greater Manchester (1989)

A police officer who had been subject to a disciplinary investigation into complaints made against him by members of the public has no right of action against his chief constable or the investigating officer for common law negligence or for breach of statutory duty based on alleged failures to conduct the disciplinary investigation properly and expeditiously. The House of Lords held that it would be contrary to public policy to recognise the existence of such a duty because there was a public interest in the full and free investigation of such complaints and the imposition of a duty of care might impede such investigations.

Lord Bridge also held that no duty is owed to civilian suspects by a police officer who is investigating a suspected crime.

European Convention for the Protection of Human Rights and Fundamental Freedoms

Following is a resumé of those articles in the Convention that are most likely to be affected by policing activities.

Article 2

Everyone's right to life shall be protected by law. No one shall be deprived of his life intentionally save in the execution of a sentence of a court following his conviction of a crime for which this penalty is provided by law.

Deprivation of life shall not be regarded as inflicted in contravention of this Article when it results from the use of force that is no more than absolutely necessary:

(a) in defence of any person from unlawful violence;

(b) in order to effect a lawful arrest or to prevent the escape of a person lawfully detained;

(c) in action lawfully taken for the purpose of quelling a riot or insurrection.

Article 3

No one shall be subjected to torture or to inhuman or degrading treatment or punishment.

Article 5

Everyone has the right to liberty and security of person. No one shall be deprived of his liberty save in the following cases and in accordance with a lawful process:

(a) the detention of a person after conviction by a competent court;

(b) the arrest or detention of a person for not complying with a court order;

(c) the arrest or detention of a person effected to bring him before a court;

(d) the detention of a minor for the purpose of educational supervision or to bring him before a court;

(e) the detention of persons for the prevention of the spreading of infectious diseases, of persons of unsound mind, alcoholics or drug addicts, or vagrants;

(f) the arrest or detention of a person to prevent his unauthorised entry into the country.

Everyone who is arrested shall be informed promptly, in a language which he understands, of the reasons for his arrest and of any charge against him and shall be brought promptly before a judge or other officer authorised by law to exercise judicial power and shall be entitled to trial within a reasonable time or to release pending trial. Release may be conditioned by guarantees to appear for trial.

Everyone who is deprived of his liberty by arrest or detention shall be entitled to take proceedings by which the lawfulness of his detention shall be decided speedily by a court and his release ordered if the detention is not lawful.

Everyone who has been the victim of arrest or detention in contravention of the provisions of this Article shall have an enforceable right to compensation.

Article 6

Everyone is entitled to a fair and public hearing within a reasonable time by an independent and impartial tribunal established by law. Judgment shall be pronounced publicly but the press and public may be excluded from all or part of the trial in the interest of morals, public order or national security in a democratic society, where the interest of juveniles or the protection of the private life of the parties so require, or to the extent strictly necessary in the opinion of the court in special circumstances where publicity would prejudice the interests of justice.

Everyone charged with a criminal offence shall be presumed innocent until proved guilty according to law and has the following minimum rights:

(a) to be informed promptly, in a language which he understands and in detail, of the nature and cause of the accusation against him;

(b) to have adequate time and facilities for the preparation of his defence;

(c) to defend himself in person or through legal assistance of his own choosing or, if he has not sufficient means to pay for legal assistance, to be given it free when the interests of justice so require;

(d) to examine or have examined witnesses against him and to obtain the attendance and examination of witnesses on his behalf under the same conditions as witnesses against him;

(e) to have the free assistance of an interpreter if he cannot understand or speak the language used in court.

Article 7

No one shall be held guilty of any criminal offence on account of any act or omission which was not a criminal offence at the time when it was committed. Nor shall a heavier penalty be imposed than the one that was applicable at the time the criminal offence was committed.

Article 8

Everyone has the right to respect for his private and family life, his home and his correspondence.

There shall be no interference by a public authority with the exercise of this right except such as is in accordance with the law and is necessary in the interests of:

- national security;
- public safety;
- the economic well-being of the country;
- the prevention of disorder or crime;
- the protection of health or morals; or
- the protection of the rights and freedoms of others.

Article 9

Everyone has the right to freedom of thought, conscience and religion. Freedom to manifest one's religion or beliefs shall be subject only to such limitations as are prescribed by law and are necessary in the interests of:

- public safety;
- the protection of public order, health or morals; or
- the protection of the rights and freedoms of others.

Article 10

Everyone has the right to freedom of expression. This right shall include freedom to hold opinions and to receive and impart information and ideas without interference by public authority and regardless of frontiers. The exercise of these freedoms, since it carries with it duties and responsibilities, may be subject to legal conditions as are necessary for:

- national security;
- territorial integrity;
- public safety;
- the prevention of disorder or crime;
- the protection of health or morals;
- the protection of the reputation or rights of others;
- preventing the disclosure of information received in confidence; or
- maintaining the authority and impartiality of the judiciary.

Article 11

Everyone has the right to freedom of peaceful assembly and to freedom of association with others. No restrictions shall be placed on the exercise of these rights except those needed for:

- national security or public safety;
- the prevention of disorder or crime;
- the protection of health or morals; or
- the protection of the rights and freedoms of others.

This Article shall not prevent the imposition of lawful restrictions on the exercise of these rights by members of the armed forces, of the police or of the administration of the state.

Article 13

Everyone whose rights and freedoms as set forth in this Convention are violated shall have an effective remedy before a national authority notwithstanding that the violation has been committed by persons acting in an official capacity.

Article 14

The enjoyment of the rights and freedoms set forth in this Convention shall be secured without discrimination on any ground such as sex, race, colour, language, religion, political or other opinion, national or social origin, association with a national minority, property, birth or other status.

19 Appendix B

Commissions and committees of inquiry affecting the governance of provincial police forces

Royal Commission on the Police 1839

This Commission was formed 'for the purpose of inquiring as to the best means of establishing an efficient constabulary force in the counties of England and Wales'.

The Commission spent nearly three years, from 1836 to 1839, in its inquiries. Amongst other things, it examined the working of Cheshire Constabulary as formed under the 1829 Act. They were not impressed by the fragmentation of the force into what was, in effect, separate constabularies in each hundred.

The Commission reported in 1839 and recommended that a single professional police force, similar to the Metropolitan Police, should be instituted to police the rural areas of England and Wales. In the event, political pressures brought about the rejection of this idea and the subsequent County Police Act 1839 bore no resemblance to the Commission's findings.

Select Committee of Parliament on the Police 1853

This Committee looked into the working of existing police arrangements throughout the country. The eventual report was brief but contained eight resolutions:

1 The 1839 permissive Act had failed to provide a general and uniform Constabulary force as is required for the prevention of crime and security of property.

2 Where the 1839 Act had been adopted, its results had been highly advantageous.

3 Superintending constables were praised for their work.

4 The continued use of parish constables was a failure, particularly for the 'poorer classes'.

5 Suggested means of adjusting the police rate to meet the circumstances of different areas.

6 The efficiency of all police forces had been impaired by lack of co-operation between rural and borough forces. It was recommended that smaller boroughs should be consolidated into the counties and larger boroughs should share management with the adjoining county, if possible under a single chief constable.

7 The government should make a contribution towards the cost of police forces without interfering with local management.

8 A recommendation that urgent legislation be enacted to make it compulsory to adopt the new police everywhere throughout the country.

Unlike many other reports most of the recommendations were implemented being enacted in the County and Borough Police Act 1856 that followed.

Royal Commission on the Police 1855

This Commission was appointed to investigate the conduct of the Metropolitan Police in a demonstration held at Hyde Park on 1 July 1855 regarding the introduction of the Sunday Trading Bill. It is of interest to note that there were about 40,000 demonstrators present and 450 police officers. The eventual report stated that the majority of the police had shown moderation and forbearance but the superintendent in Hyde Park had 'lost his head' and certain officers had been guilty of unnecessary violence.

Select Committee on the House of Commons 1875

During the late 1860s and early 1870s a series of disquieting revelations came to light regarding the use of police superannuation funds. Additionally, it was evident that the payment of pensions to retired police officers was by no means universal, nor was the rate of pension at a standard level.

This Committee recommended that police should be awarded a pension as a matter of right after 25 years' service, that pension rates should be the same throughout the country and that they should be a direct charge on local rates. Eventually, after 15 years of effort these recommendations were embodied in the Police Act 1890.

Royal Commission on the Police 1906

The Commission was set up to inquire into the handling of 'street offences' – prostitution, drunken and disorderly behaviour and street betting in the Metropolitan Police area. The Commission took two years to report, and when it did, it exonerated the Metropolitan Police of practically all of the charges of corruption and malpractice that had been made, nine instances of 'reprehensible conduct' being recorded. The Metropolitan Police Force was totally vindicated by what was, in fact, an anti-police, politically inspired Commission.

Select Committee on the Employment of the Military in Cases of Disturbance 1908

This Committee reported on the use of troops in situations of disorder and commented particularly on two cases in which they had opened fire on the rioters.

The Committee recommended that the Home Secretary should be given the power to requisition up to 10% of the officers of any county force and direct them to any area threatened by riot. The recommendation was not adopted, however, a subsequent Home Secretary did send Metropolitan Police officers to South Wales to deal with rioting in preference to the use of troops.

Select Committee on Police Hours of Work 1908

During 1906–07 there was discontent over the fact that police officers were not entitled to either time off during the working week nor to any holiday break during the year. The recommendations of this Committee were accepted and embodied in the Police Forces (Weekly Rest Day) Act 1910.

Committee of Inquiry 1919 (Desborough)

This Inquiry was set up to consider and report whether any and what changes should be made in the method of recruiting for, the conditions of service of, and the rates of pay, pensions and allowances of the police forces of England, Wales and Scotland.

The Inquiry was set up in answer to the industrial unrest that was being instigated by National Union of Police and Prison Officers and in consequence the report was made in two parts.

The first part of the report dealt with pay and conditions and formed the basis of the Police Act 1919. The second part of the report dealt with the organisation and administration of provincial police forces, many of which were implemented by administrative rather than legislative action.

Royal Commission on Police Powers and Proceedures 1929 (Lee)

This Commission was instituted following the arrest in Hyde Park of a well-known financier and a young woman for an obscure by-law offence relating to indecency. The case was dismissed, but certain left wing MPs pursued the question of 'police brutality and corruption' until the Commission was set up to inquire into the procedures for interviewing suspects and taking statements (the 'Judge's Rules').

The Commission made no recommendations that were implemented, but they did give their opinion about the status of a constable which is to be found in Chapter 2 of this handbook. The description used by the Commission is not original, it was originally published in a law book of 1883!

Committee of Inquiry 1948 (Oaksey)

After the repeal of the Police and Firemen (War Service) Act 1939 and the inevitable exodus of many long service police officers, all police forces, especially those in London and the larger cities were faced with enormous manpower shortages. Work was fairly easy to find, tended to be better paid and had none of the restrictions that police regulations imposed. Matters were approaching crisis proportions when the government set up a committee to consider the need for recruitment and retention of an adequate number of suitable men and women for the police forces of England, Wales and Scotland, and to report on pay, emoluments, allowances, pensions, promotion, methods of representation and negotiation, and other conditions of service.

The *Desborough Report* had examined the same area and had recommended pay scales that had put police officers amongst the best paid of the blue collar workers. However, in the intervening period police pay had fallen significantly behind that of other workers.

As with *Desborough* the *Oaksey Report* was made in two parts. The first dealing with pay, pensions and conditions of service, the second dealing with training, promotion discipline and other kindred matters.

The hopes of the Committee had little chance of success as too little was offered in the existing economic climate. In 1919 police officers had resorted to strike action but in the years between *Oaksey* and *Edmund-Davies* they voted with their feet and left the job in large numbers. Most forces had an enormous turnover of staff, the majority of recruits leaving with under four years' service. This led to chronic deficiencies in most police forces of between 18 and 20% of the authorised establishment. In some forces the deficiency was as high as a quarter of the establishment.

Royal Commission on the Police 1960 (Willink)

The starting point of this inquiry involved the actor Brian Rix who was stopped for speeding and a civil servant named Garratt who stopped and interfered in the incident. He was arrested but the charge was refused by the duty inspector. Subsequently, Garratt instituted a writ for damages against the police officer and the matter was settled out of court for £300.

A year after the event it was discussed in the House of Commons and much was made of police accountability and the rights of individual citizens. Several incidents of police misconduct that had occurred over the previous 10 years were resurrected in the debates which eventually resulted in the setting up of another Royal Commission.

The terms of reference included:

- the constitution and functions of local police authorities;
- the status and accountability of all members of police forces, including chief officers of police;
- the relationship of the police with the public and the means of ensuring that complaints by the public against the police are effectively dealt with;
- the 'broad principles' which should determine the level of police pay having regard to the nature and extent of police duties and responsibilities and the need to attract and retain an adequate number of recruits with proper qualifications.

The Royal Commission produced Part I of its report which related to police pay. However it went further than merely outlining principles by proposing actual pay scales.

The Royal Commission report said:

> We do not think that anyone acquainted with the facts can be satisfied with the state of law and order in Great Britain in 1960 … police pay is at present inadequate either to inspire in the police and the community a sense of fair treatment, or to attract to the service as a whole and retain in it, enough recruits of the right standard.

The new scales were paid, but, for economic reasons, they soon fell behind the level of pay outside the service. After about two years the problem of recruitment and retention was as bad as it had ever been.

Part II of the report was of far greater significance in the longer term. A number of recommendations were made regarding police accountability and control and these were strongly debated in Parliament. Eventually the Police Act 1964 was enacted which brought about the wholesale restructuring of the provincial police forces in England and Wales.

Committee of Inquiry on the Police 1978 (Edmund-Davies)

For various economic reason, particularly high inflation, starting with the Fire Brigades in 1977, a series of strikes were called in the public sector. This ultimately led to the so-called 'winter of discontent' in 1978–79 and the defeat of the Labour government in a general election in May 1979.

Police were as discontented as other public service workers and increasing numbers were leaving the service. In 1978 the government appointed a committee under Lord Edmund-Davies with terms restricted to:

reviewing the constitutions of the machinery for negotiating police pay and examining the constitutions of police staff associations.

This did not satisfy police and there were calls for the ban on strike action to be repealed. The government then reluctantly renamed the body's title to the 'Committee of Inquiry on the Police' and extended the terms of reference to include: 'a study of the proper basis of police pay'.

The report was issued in July 1978 and, for the first time since 1829 the criteria for police pay was established. Both press and the public in general received the report favourably, possibly because of the anxiety over the widespread industrial action that continued. The government was less favourably disposed and decided to implement the pay recommendation in two stages with a 12 month gap between them. Following the general election in May 1979 the new government reversed the staging decision and immediately put in hand steps for police to receive the new rates of pay.

This report had an almost immediate effect on police establishments by reducing the numbers of officers resigning early, whilst recruiting stayed at more or less the same level. Within a few years police establishments, for the first time since the Second World War, showed few deficiencies, although it must be said that increasing unemployment also played a part

Royal Commission on Criminal Procedure 1977 (Phillips)

In 1972 a transvestite prostitute named Maxwell Confait was killed when his house was set on fire. Subsequently three youths were charged with his murder – Lattimore, 18 years old but with a mental age of eight, Leighton, 15 years old but borderline subnormal and Salih, 14 years old. The three were convicted of manslaughter and their appeals were rejected on the basis of admissions that they had made in respect of the arson attack.

Subsequently, the Home Secretary referred the case back to the Court of Appeal for reconsideration. Medical evidence, not given at the trial, proved the time of Confait's death and the boys could not have been present at that time.

At the appeal, Lord Scarman said that the effect of this fresh medical evidence was to 'destroy the lynch-pin of the Crown's case and to demonstrate that the version of events contained in the admissions relied upon by the Crown cannot be true'.

An Inquiry was held into the taking of the statements under a High Court Judge but the result was equivocal. Later, more medical and other evidence confirmed the innocence of the three boys.

The next step occurred in June 1977 when a Royal Commission was set up with the following terms of reference:

To examine, having regard both to the interests of the community in bringing offenders to justice and the rights and liberties of persons suspected of crime, and taking into account also the need for efficient and economical use of resources, whether changes are needed in England and Wales in:

- the powers and duties of the police in respect of the investigation of criminal offences and the rights and duties of suspect and accused persons, including the means by which they are secured;
- the process of and responsibility for the prosecution of criminal offences; and
- such other features of criminal procedure and evidence as relate to the above

and to make recommendations in these matters.

The Royal Commission reported in January 1981 and as a direct result of the recommendations it was followed by the Police and Criminal Evidence Act 1984.

Inquiry on the Brixton Disorders 1981 (Scarman)

This Inquiry was set up to examine the Brixton and other disorders that had occurred in 1981. Scarman made a number of recommendations that were directly associated with the police handling of the disorder and amongst them was a recommendation that police authorities and chief constables should establish arrangements for community involvement and consultative arrangements with communities. This recommendation was given statutory authority in the Police and Criminal Evidence Act 1984.

House of Commons Home Affairs Select Committee on the Working of Police Special Branches 1985

Following public disquiet about the activities of police special branches the Select Committee inquired into their activities. The eventual report was coloured by party politics with the Conservative majority producing a report that said public disquiet was unfounded and the Labour members produced a minority report that indicated there was some cause for concern. The one matter of significance that resulted from the Inquiry was the publication by the Home Secretary of Guidelines on Special Branch Work in Great Britain in December 1984. This was the first time that such information had been put into the public domain.

Inquiry into Police Responsibilities and Rewards 1993 (Sheehy)

This Inquiry was set up to examine the rank structure, remuneration and conditions of service of the police service. The avowed objective of the Inquiry team was to put the police service on a 'businesslike' footing and to this end all five of its members had business experience but none of them had any direct knowledge of policing.

The recommendations when published were strongly criticised from all sections of the police service and some chief officers threatened to resign if the recommendations were implemented in full. Sheehy for his part said that the police should not pick and choose, the package had to be accepted *in toto*. In the event, the Home Secretary eventually rejected most of the radical recommendations but accepted some of the less contentious points such as the reduction in the number of police ranks, the buying out of inspectors' overtime rights and placing chief officers on short-term, renewable contracts associated with evaluation of their performance.

20 Appendix C

A brief 'legal' history of the police force

The first policing statute was enacted in 1285, see Chapter 1 for details. The modern legislation came at the beginning of the 19th century since when over 60 policing statutes have been passed by Parliament. Some of these Acts have introduced innovations in the manner of administering the police forces in England and Wales whilst others have made little more than cosmetic changes to the then existing conditions.

Following is a list of the most important of these statutes with brief details of the subject matter of each one.

Statue of Winchester 1285

Directed that the 'Hue and Cry' should be raised to pursue criminals. Ordered that towns should arrange a watch and ward system of policing.

Improvement Acts 1750 (and later)

From 1750 onwards, due to increasing crime and disorder in the urban areas, about 200 towns promoted their own Improvement Acts of Parliament. The details of these Acts varied considerably, but all authorised the raising of a local rate and the appointment of paid *improvement commissioners*. The commissioners oversaw such things as street paving and lighting and in most cases they appointed and paid a *night watch* who were sworn in as constables. A very small number were also appointed as day constables.

In reality, the Improvement Acts were used as a means of discharging the duties defined in the Statute of Winchester 1285, by paying individuals to undertake the duties that were imposed on all citizens.

Cheshire Police Act 1829

This Act was passed a month before the Metropolitan Police Act of the same year. It was considered, at the time, to be the prototype policing system that could be used nationally for all county police forces. The Act provided for:

- Each hundred in the county to have a stipendiary deputy high constable. (Nine such officials were appointed.)
- Each high constable, under the authority of the local magistrates, was given control of several paid petty constables.

Cheshire thus became the first area outside London and a few other large towns to maintain a regular 'professional' constabulary.

Metropolitan Police Act 1829

This Act was introduced to 'improve the Police in and near the Metropolis'.

It authorised the swearing in as Justices (later called Commissioners) of two fit persons to create and administer a police force composed of a sufficient number of fit and able men.

The Justices (Commissioners) were empowered to direct and control the force under the authority of the Home Secretary. They were also given the power to frame orders for the government of the force subject to the approval of the Home Secretary.

This Act separated the administration of policing from the control of the local justices of the peace and parishes for the first time and it remains the governing statute of the Metropolitan Police to the present day.

Special Constables Act 1831

This Act empowered justices of the peace to conscript men as special constables on the occasion of riot or threat of riot. This Act was passed following the serious riots that occurred in several towns and cities during the passage of the Reform Bill through Parliament.

Lighting and Watching Act 1833

This was the first Act to deal in general with paid police outside London. It empowered parishes to levy a rate and appoint police who could be sworn in as constables. It was not mandatory and ratepayers could adopt its provisions if they so wished. It is not known how many parishes actually made use of the powers in the Act.

Municipal Corporations Act 1835

This Act required chartered* boroughs in England and Wales to establish police forces. Any police force maintained under the Lighting and Watching Act 1833 was replaced by the newly authorised police force.

All new councils elected under the terms of this Act *had* to form a *Watch Committee*.

Watch Committees were directed to appoint a sufficient number of fit men to be sworn in as constables for preserving the peace by day and night and preventing robberies. They were also empowered to make appointment, dismiss and to make regulations for the governance of their police force.

This Act preserved the common law powers of a constable and gave statutory force to the old convention that he should obey the lawful commands of a justice of the peace.

* 'Chartered' boroughs had been incorporated by past royal charters and did not include many newly industrialised areas such as Manchester and Birmingham that had not been incorporated. There was no obligation on these industrial areas to establish police forces.

Metropolitan Police Act 1836

This Act embodied the Bow Street Horse Patrol into the Metropolitan Police where it became the Mounted Branch.

City of London Police Act 1838

This Act established the City of London Police Force under the command of a commissioner appointed by, and answerable to, the Corporation of the City of London.

Metropolitan Police Act 1839

This act extended the boundaries of the Metropolitan Police. It converted the River Thames Police into the Thames Division of the Metropolitan Police and absorbed the Bow Street Foot Patrol into the Metropolitan Police. The Act also stopped the direct employment of constables by magistrates in the Metropolitan area.

County Police Act 1839

This Act *permitted*, but did not require, magistrates in Quarter Sessions to establish a police force, with the consent of the Home Secretary, for the whole of a county, or for a particular part of it.

The number of constables employed were not to exceed the ratio of one constable to 1,000 head of population and all appointments were in the hands of the Magistracy.

The Home Secretary was given power to make regulations regarding the government of and pay of constables. His approval was also required for the appointment of the chief constable of a force authorised by this Act.

Those counties affected by political and industrial unrest, largely fomented by the Chartists, adopted the Act, either for the whole of the county or a specific part of it. These forces became relatively efficient within a fairly short period of time. Other counties, unaffected by large-scale disorder, ignored the Act and took no steps towards the provision of a professional police force.

County Police Act 1840

This Act stipulated that any police force constituted under the Lighting and Watching Act 1833 should be discontinued upon the chief constable of the county undertaking to take charge of the district.

Parish Constables Act 1842

This Act re-affirmed the obligation of each community to police itself. Justices were required to hold special sessions for the purpose of compiling lists of fit male ratepayers of good character between the ages of 25 and 55 who were to be sworn in as parish constables. The old practice of paying substitutes to carry out the parish constable duties was legalised and parishes were empowered to appoint paid constables as an alternative to using unpaid ratepayers.

The Act also created a different form of paid constable called a super-intending constable who was paid from the county rate and was to have control over the parish constables in his petty sessional division.

This Act was a sop to county authorities who had complained that the 'new' police forces created under the County Police Act 1839 were too expensive.

Town Police Clauses Act 1847

This Act provided prescribed model conditions for adoption by those police forces provided under Improvement Acts of Parliament in those towns that did not come within the ambit of the Municipal Corporations Act 1835.

County and Borough Police Act 1856

This Act required all counties to establish rural police forces.

County constables would have the same jurisdiction in boroughs that borough men had always had in the counties.

The Act authorised the appointment of three HM Inspectors of Constabulary to assess the efficiency of all police forces in England and Wales.

An Exchequer grant equal to a quarter of the cost of the wages and uniform of men employed in a police force would be payable, subject to the force being certified as being efficient. No grant was payable in respect of any police force that served a population of under 5,000 people.

Police authorities were required to submit statistics on crime in the police area to the Home Secretary.

Parish Constables Act 1872

The Parish Constables Act 1842 was a complete failure and in this Act it was stated that as the establishment of efficient police forces in the counties of England and Wales had rendered the general appointment of parish constables unnecessary, no more will be appointed in future, unless the justices in quarter sessions so ordered.

Police (Expenses) Act 1874

This Act increased the Exchequer grant paid to forces from one-quarter to one-half of the authorised expenditure.

Municipal Corporations (New Charters) Act 1877

This Act stipulated that no scheme for the incorporation of a borough would be allowed to include the formation of a separate police force unless the population exceeded 20,000. The Act did not affect existing police forces whose police area had a population under 20,000.

Local Government Act 1888

This Act abolished separate police forces in towns with a population under 10,000 people.

Standing joint committees were introduced as police authorities for county forces.

The Home Secretary was given power to give directions to police authorities to ensure the maintenance of proper standards of discipline, efficiency and establishment in county police forces.

Police Act 1890

Police pensions introduced on a formal basis for time serving officers, for policemen injured on duty and for the widows of officers killed on duty.

The Act also authorised standing agreements made between particular forces to provide mutual aid to each other when needed.

Police Forces (Weekly Rest-Day) Act 1910

This Act authorised police officers having one day's leave in each seven.

Police Act 1919

This was a milestone Act that standardised pay and conditions for all police officers in every force throughout the country.

To cover the additional cost to local ratepayers the defined terms of authorised expenditure were widened thus increasing the amounts paid in the Exchequer grant.

Serving police officers were barred from being members of trade unions and the Act established the Police Federation and created the Police Council as a consultative body.

The Act also allowed the appointment of chief constables from outside the police service if the applicant had 'exceptional qualifications or experience'.

The Act authorised the Home Secretary to make regulations concerning all police forces. Thus for the first time he was able to lay down some national standards by law.

Emergency Powers (Defence) Act 1939

This Act authorised the making of regulations covering any imaginable matter. They were referred to as the Defence Regulations and were enforceable until 1945 at the end of the Second World War. Some of the regulations were subsequently embodied into other peacetime legislation.

Regulations empowered the Home Secretary to amalgamate any two or more police areas if it was considered necessary for facilitating naval, military or air operations.

Several amalgamations took place in areas defined as being 'liable to invasion or which were important in relation to offensive military operations', all of which arrangements were subsequently confirmed in the Police Act 1946.

Police and Firemen (War Service) Act 1939

This Act provided that any person employed as a constable must continue in employment until his/her services were dispensed with by the Home Secretary or chief constable. When this Act was repealed it led to chronic undermanning in all police forces which lasted until 1980 after the implementation of the *Edmund-Davies Report* recommendations.

Police (His Majesty's Inspectors of Constabulary) Act 1945

This Act placed the duties, establishment and organisation of HM Inspectors of Constabulary, who had existed since 1856, on a formal legal footing.

Police Act 1946

This Act abolished non-county borough police forces.

Compulsory amalgamation powers were given to the Home Secretary when they were needed in the interests of efficiency of police forces covering a population of less than 100,000 people. Forces were also permitted to make voluntary merging arrangements.

Miscellaneous Finance Provisions Act 1950

The Police Grant Order, 1951 made under section 3 of this Act placed the payment of the police grant on a statutory basis for the first time.

The Order permitted the payment of the grant, subject to the conditions that:

- the area was efficiently policed;
- adequate co-operation was afforded to other police forces;
- the force was efficiently and properly maintained, equipped and administered;
- the rates of pay and allowances were as laid down by the Home Secretary.

Police Act 1964

Another milestone Act that brought about a complete revision and re-enactment of the whole of the law concerning the governance and control of police forces.

The Act attempted to define the respective functions of the Home Secretary, police authorities and chief constables.

Chief constables were given the powers of appointment, discipline and promotion over subordinates and they were designated as having 'control and direction' of their police force.

The Home Secretary was given the duty of taking initiatives to promote the efficiency of the police and the powers necessary to implement that duty. This included the power to recommend or, if necessary, enforce police force amalgamations into larger units.

The Act increased the functions of HM Inspectorate of Constabulary and also put on a statutory footing such things as common police services.

The Police Council, set up under the 1919 Act was replaced by the Police Advisory Council to advise the Home Secretary on general questions affecting the Service. The Police Council for Great Britain was recognised as the official negotiating body for the Police Service.

It provided for the complete or partial repeal of 61 Acts of Parliament dating back to the early 19th century, some of which are shown above.

Following the passing into law of the 1964 Act the Home Secretary, using his new powers, recommended and in some cases enforced a series of amalgamations and mergers that reduced the number of police forces from 117 to 49.

Local Government Act 1972

This Act reformed local government boundaries throughout England and Wales and stated that policing was to be the responsibility of the new county councils, except in those cases of existing combined forces that policed more than one county. Some counties were to be amalgamated to secure efficient policing to modern standards.

The Act resulted in a further round of changes of police force boundaries.

Police Act 1976

This Act set up the Police Complaints Board.

Chief constables were required to send all complaints to the Board unless investigation has resulted in disciplinary hearings, or, after reference to the Director of Public Prosecutions, criminal proceedings.

Police and Criminal Evidence Act 1984

This Act reviewed and placed upon a statutory footing the procedures to be followed by police officers when dealing with suspected or arrested persons. There were provisions relating to the giving of evidence in criminal proceedings.

The Act also laid down procedures for the handling of complaints and disciplinary proceedings against police officers.

It also required police authorities after consultation with their chief constables to make arrangements for obtaining the views of the people in their police area concerning policing.

Security Service Act 1989

This Act placed the Security Service on a statutory basis and defined the controls and supervision over its operations.

Police and Magistrates' Courts Act 1994

This Act made substantial reforms to the structure of the Police Service in England and Wales designed to improve its management and organisation to make it better able to combat crime.

The most significant changes related to the formation of police authorities who were taken out of the direct control of county councils and made into independent corporate bodies that have some similarities to the old standing joint committees of counties prior to 1964.

Criminal Justice and Public Order Act 1994

This Act authorised cross border arrests between English and Welsh police forces, Scottish police forces and the Royal Ulster Constabulary.

The Act also authorised mutual aid arrangements between the same police forces.

Police Act 1996

This Act consolidated the legislation in respect of the governance of police forces in England and Wales.

The Act did not alter the law but brought together all of the statutory provisions from 1964 onward and presented them in a single statute.

Security Service Act 1996

This Act extended the functions of the Security Service to include actions in support of the police in connection with the prevention and detection of serious crime.

Police (Health and Safety) Act 1997

This Act extends the provisions of the Health and Safety at Work Act 1974 to members of police forces.

Police Act 1997

The main points of this Act were to put the National Criminal Intelligence Service and the National Crime Squad on a statutory footing and to lay down controls over the use of surveillance equipment by the police.

21 Bibliography

During the compilation of this handbook a number of documents were consulted and following is a restricted list of the most important of them. Also listed are some titles that I feel would be useful to a reader who wished to study particular topics in greater detail. Additionally, several contemporary newspaper reports were also consulted.

Law sources

Statutes

Health and Safety at Work Act 1974 as later amended.
Police and Criminal Evidence Act 1984 as later amended.
Security Service Act 1989
Criminal Justice and Public Order Act 1994
Police Act 1996
Security Service Act 1996
Police (Health and Safety) Act 1997
Police Act 1997

Blackstone's Statute Books

Ghandhi, PR, *International Human Rights Documents*, 1st edn, 1995.
Wallington, P and Lee, RG, *Statutes on Public Law*, 6th edn, 1996–97.

Other statute reference

Elagab, OY, *International Law Documents Relating to Terrorism*, 2nd edn 1997, London: Cavendish Publishing Ltd.
Stone's Justices' Manual (annual publication), London: Butterworth & Co Ltd.

Case reports

Law reports in *The Times* and *The Independent* newspapers.
Law Updates (annually, 1993–97) London: HLT Publications.
Kidner, R, *Casebook on Torts*, 4th edn, 1996, London: Blackstone Press Ltd.

Books consulted

Ackroyd, C, Margolis, K, Rosenhead, J and Shallice, T, *The Technology of Political Control*, 1977, Harmondsworth: Penguin Books Ltd.

Allason, R, *The Branch: A History of the Metropolitan Police Special Branch 1883–1983*, 1983, London: Secker and Warburg.

Ascoli, D, *The Queen's Peace*, 1979, London: Hamish Hamilton.

Aubrey, C, *Who's watching you?*, 1981, Harmondsworth: Penguin Books Ltd.

Audit Commission Police Papers as listed on pages 101–02.

Bailey, SH, Harris, DJ and Jones, BL, *Civil Liberties: Cases and Materials*, 3rd edn, 1991, London: Butterworth & Co Ltd.

Baker, CD, *Tort*, 5th edn, 1991, London: Sweet & Maxwell.

Bunyan, T, *The Political Police in Britain*, 1976, reprinted 1983, London: Quartet Books.

Campbell, D, *Phonetappers and the Security State*, Report 2, 1981, London: New Statesman.

Cane, P, *An Introduction to Administrative Law*, 1986, Oxford: Clarendon Press. (Now out of date in parts, but gives good explanations.)

Cox, B, *Civil Liberties in Britain*, 1975, Harmondsworth: Penguin Books Ltd.

Critchley, TA, *A History of Police in England and Wales*, 1979, London: Constable.

De Smith, S and Brazier, R, *Constitutional and Administrative Law*, 7th edn, 1994, London: Penguin Books Ltd.

Ewing, KD and Gearty, GA, *Freedom under Thatcher: Civil Liberties in Modern Britain*, 1990, Oxford: Clarendon Press.

Fenwick, H, *Civil Liberties*, 3rd edn, 1998, London: Cavendish Publishing Ltd.

Gifford, Lord, *Report into Political Policing in Wales*, 1984, Welsh Campaign for Civil and Political Liberties.

Hain, P, *Political Trials in Britain*, 1985, Harmondsworth: Penguin Books Ltd.

Harpwood, V, *Principles of Tort Law*, 3rd edn, 1997, London: Cavendish Publishing Ltd.

Home Office, *Review of Police Core and Ancillary tasks*, 1995, London: HMSO.

James, RW, *To The Best of Our Skill and Knowledge*, 1957, Cheshire Constabulary.

Lea, J and Young, J, *What is to be done about Law and Order*, 1984, Harmondsworth: Penguin Books Ltd.

Lustgarten, L, *The Governance of Police*, 1986, London: Sweet & Maxwell.

Mark, R, *In the Office of Constable*, 1978, London: Collins.

McCrudden, C and Chambers, G, *Individual Rights and the Law in Britain*, 1994, The Law Society, Oxford: Clarendon Press.

Morton, J, *Bent Coppers*, 1994, London: Warner Books.

Oliver, I, *Police, Government and Accountability*, 2nd edn, 1997, London: Macmillan Press Ltd.

Reiner, R, *Chief Constables: Bobbies, Bosses or Bureaucrats?*, 1991, Oxford: Oxford University Press.

Reiner, R, *The Politics of the Police*, 1992, London: Harvester Wheatsheaf.

Reynolds, GW and Judge, A, *The Night the Police went on Strike*, 1968, London: Weidenfeld and Nicolson.

Robertson, G, *Freedom, the Individual and the Law*, 1989, London: Penguin Books Ltd.

Scarman, Lord, *Report of an Inquiry into the Brixton Disorders 10–12 April 1981*, 1982, Harmondsworth: Penguin Books Ltd.

Scraton, P, *The State of the Police*, 1985, London: Pluto Press.

Sellwood, AV, *Police Strike – 1919*, 1978, London: WH Allen.

Thackrah, JR, *Contemporary Policing: An Examination of Society in the 1980s*, 1985, London: Sphere Reference.

Thompson, SP, *Maintaining the Queen's Peace*, 1958, Birkenhead Borough Police.

Waud, C, *Employment Law 1995*, 1995, Daily Telegraph, London: Kogan Page.

Whitaker, B, *The Police*, 1964, Harmondsworth: Penguin Special.

Willinck, Sir Henry, *Report by the Royal Commission on the Police*, 1962, London: HMSO.

Index